M000003915

Collaboration

with the Divine

A SACRED COMMUNION

Women's Sacred Stories

Freedom House Publishing Co.

Collaboration with the Divine

A SACRED COMMUNION

Copyright © 2022

All rights reserved. No part of this publication may be reproduced, stored in a retrieval system, or transmitted in any for or by any means, electronic, mechanical, photocopying, recording, or otherwise, without written permission of the publisher or author, except for the use of brief quotations in a book review.

Although the author and publisher have made every effort to ensure that the information in this book was correct at press time, the author and publisher do not assume and hereby disclaim any liability to any party for any loss, damage, or disruption caused by errors or omissions, whether such errors or omissions result from negligence, accident, or any other cause.

Adherence to all applicable laws and regulations, including international, federal, state and local governing professional licensing, business practices, advertising, and all other aspects of doing business in the US, Canada or any other jurisdiction is the sole responsibility of the reader and consumer.

Neither the author nor the publisher assumes any responsibility or liability whatsoever on behalf of the consumer or reader of this material. Any perceived slight of any individual or organization is purely unintentional.

The resources in this book are provided for informational purposes only and should not be used to replace the specialized training and professional judgment of a health care or mental health care professional.

Neither the author nor the publisher can be held responsible for the use of the information provided within this book. Please always consult a trained professional before making any decision regarding treatment of yourself or others.

To request permissions, contact the publisher at
freedomhousepublishingco@gmail.com

Paperback ISBN: 978-1-952566-41-7
978-1-952566-43-1
Ebook ISBN: 978-1-952566-42-4
Printed in the USA.
Freedom House Publishing Co
Middleton, ID 83644
www.freedomhousepublishingco.com

FREEDOM HOUSE
PUBLISHING CO

TABLE OF CONTENTS

THE PURPOSE

This book is here to assist you in your own experience of collaborating and communing with the Divine. Each chapter will guide you through an author's experience of connecting to the Divine and what has transpired in their life.

This book is here to be a reminder to all humans that the Divine is real; that you are known, loved, and seen by the Divine. That even with 7.9 billion people on this earth, you are known. You are loved. And you can connect, collaborate, and commune with the Divine— *no matter who you are.*

That is the purpose of this book. But it was a different purpose that actually called this book into existence—and that is a nonprofit that I have created called Centers of Hope.

This nonprofit directly serves individuals who are struggling with depression and suicidal ideation. The Center of Hope will be a physical building constructed with light as the focus. Each building will be created to bring safety, security, light, and specific plans of healing for each individual who enters through the doors. These centers will be filling a massive hole in the world right now. Suicide is one of the leading causes of death in the world, but there are very few resources that truly support those who are struggling. My desire is to create centers that feel safe, warm, loving, and filled with light for those who are pulling themselves out of the darkest places.

We will be combining the worlds of psychiatrics and medicine with the energy healing world of Reiki, energy work, Rapid Eye Therapy, Sound Healing, and more.

There is no right way to support an individual who struggles with suicide ideation. There are many different ways, and, at each center, individuals will be able to find the method that works for them and create a plan of action towards healing and living.

This book is just the beginning of raising the funds necessary for these physical buildings. Each author in this book invested their own money to become a co-author, and all of their investment funds have begun the process for these centers to come to fruition. Plus, all of the proceeds from this book will go directly towards the Centers of Hope.

If you would like to support this powerful cause, I invite you to check out our website www.centersofhope.org and donate what you can.

It is my belief that those who struggle with suicidal ideation are the brightest lights on this planet. They are here to be changemakers, healers, leaders, creators, and more! So, the darkness works the hardest on them. In many cases, suicide takes them before they are able to bless the world with their light.

I am fighting for these brilliant beings. I am fighting for them to be released from the darkness that wants to snuff out their light. I envision the Centers of Hope being in every city of America. And soon, globally.

It is time that we fight for these brave warriors of light and show them that there is way out of the darkness. I invite you to join me on this powerful journey of light. Join me in sharing this book, donating to our efforts, and being a light in your own beautiful and powerful way.

For many, the path to knowing the Divine is a rocky and turbulent one. For a lot of people, awakening to know the Divine has only come when they have hit the lowest and darkest place in their lives.

As sweet and joyous as it is to collaborate with the Divine, the process to truly untether ourselves from our humanity and welcome spiritual communion can be painful.

There will be stories within this book that share the author's painful awakening that led them to knowing the Divine. These stories are raw and real. They can also be triggering for some readers. I believe that sharing the whole story is how we feel seen in our own pain and our own turbulent path. But I also want to respect each reader for where they are and I do not want this book to open any wounds that the reader may not be ready to heal.

For this purpose, I will be placing an image of a phoenix bird at the end of a chapter title of any story that deals with triggering topics. I chose this image because the story of a phoenix resembles the path that these authors have walked.

A phoenix is a symbol of death and rebirth. As the phoenix dies in a flame of fire, it then rebirths from those ashes, stronger and more brilliant than ever before.

There are chapters within this book that will dive into deep and heavy topics, such as abuse, suicidal ideation, suicide attempts, and more. Each one of these stories share the authors' walk through their own fire and how they came out stronger and more alive.

While these stories are massively impactful and deeply important, I do want to respect you, as the reader, so that you feel safe as you read this book, and that you venture only into the chapters that you feel comfortable reading.

I honor each story that is within the pages of this book as sacred work. This book is sacred work.

I am grateful you are here with us on this miraculous journey of collaborating with the Divine, a sacred communion.

Thank you,

Keira

Chapter 1

COLLABORATION AND COMMUNION

By: Keira Poulsen

C ollaboration—this is a word we hear often. In the marketing space, it is used daily as businesses, entrepreneurs, and social media influencers connect together to share each other's work with the world. In my opinion, this word is a bit tired and overused.

But there is a different feeling when this word is connected to the Divine.

The true definition of collaboration is: "The action of working with someone to produce or create something." I would like to substitute the word "someone" with the Divine to make the new definition: "The action of working with *the Divine* to produce or create something."

That is the definition of what *this book* is about. It is a compilation of multiple women and their stories of collaborating with the Divine.

This book is a witness. It is a witness that the Divine is real; that God is real. And not only is God real, God know us, sees us, and will work with us if we are open to receive such powerful communion.

This book is a witness that the Divine Mother is real. She knows us down to the very cells of our beings. She is always here, ready to envelop us in Her love. Her warmth and tenderness await our willingness to connect with Her.

This book is a witness that there are ascended masters who can support us in our lives. Christ, Buddha, Mother Isis, Kuan Yin, and more. We have angels who are a part of our spiritual team. They are standing by, waiting for us to invite them to participate in our creations, our struggles, and our lives. The Divine is your spiritual team.

For each author, the Divine shows up differently. Every one of us connects differently to the Divine, and we each hear and receive the Divine in our own ways. There is not one particular way to hear, receive, or work with the Divine.

I believe it is because we all have different spiritual gifts. While my spiritual gift is the gift of seeing and receiving visions, others have the gifts of hearing, feeling, sensing, knowing, and more. Your gifts will help you receive from the Divine.

As you read through each author's story in this book, my hope and desire is that you will find yourselves in one or more of these chapters. I hope that as you hear all of the different ways these women have connected to the Divine, it will become clear that there is no right or wrong way to hear divinity.

I also believe in the power of witness. One of the most frustrating aspects of being a human who desires spiritual connection is that when we have spiritual experiences, our mind likes to negate or doubt them. I remember as a teenager hearing a quote that has stuck with me my whole life. It went something like this: "A spiritual moment is like a moonbeam. It leaves as quickly as it comes."

I have seen this happen in my life time and time again. A spiritual experience would come into my world but would leave quickly with an aftertaste of doubt. The doubt robs us of the joy that came with the spiritual connection that we just experienced.

I know this is not just my personal experience. We can see it in many biblical stories as God would send multiple witnesses to those with whom He was connecting. We see it in the birth story of Christ. After Mary had her spiritual experience with God, an angel came to Joseph to witness of what had happened with Mary. And again, after the birth of Christ, an angel appeared to the shepherds, telling them to go and see the Christ child. Later, the wisemen visited Mary and Joseph to worship their little one.

I have often thought how easy it would've been for Mary and Joseph to question if this baby, who looked like all the other babies, was indeed the Christ. How easy would it have been to tell themselves that they had made up their experiences? I would imagine that doubt would've been pretty loud as they raised this child like every other parent in their town. Dirty diapers, sleepless nights, tantrums… it would've been very easy to doubt. But God sent multiple witnesses to remind them of the Divinity of their son and His purpose.

Whether or not you are Christian and believe this story doesn't really matter. It is an example of the purpose of witness. Our minds have a tendency to lean towards doubt when it comes to the realm of spirituality. Facts and reality are easier for our minds to compute and believe. But, when we can share our spiritual experiences with others, something powerful takes place. It becomes a witness to our minds. The spiritual experience no longer slips out of our fingers like a moonbeam, but instead becomes as real as the dirt below our feet.

As we share our experiences with those who have a willingness to receive, a witness occurs for those who hear and for those who share. And that is what this book is here to do. It is here to breathe life into each story that is shared. This book is here to remind you of all the times you have connected to the Divine. Big moments or small, these memories will resurface like treasures from the past. As they do, I invite you to write them down. Bring them to the earth and allow them to breathe, and then share them with those who you know can receive them.

That is an important aspect I want to acknowledge—be wise with whom you share your spiritual experiences with. These experiences are delicate and brittle at first. They will become strong and eventually unbreakable but, at first, when you start to see them and experience them, it is very important that you use wisdom in whom you share with.

If you share one of these treasured moments with someone who has no belief in the Divine, or doubts all spiritual connection, then they cannot hold the space for the sacredness of which you are sharing. And it can be devastating to share something so tender and sweet only to have it rejected and its validity denied.

There will come a time when you are so strong in your own belief of your experiences that you can share with anyone at any time and no one can deter you. But as you grow your muscle of spiritual receiving, it is imperative that you treat these sacred experiences like new flower shoots straight from the earth. Love them, care for them, and share them with those you know can receive them with love.

You can do this by simply writing down every experience that comes to you. Bring it earthbound. The writing will amplify its power and truth. And then share the experience when you feel inspired to share. This simple practice will invite more spiritual experiences into your life. They will grow stronger and stronger and will show up more often than you could ever imagine.

I have a deep love for the spiritual realm. It is the core and root of my life. I have found great comfort in spending time with God, my Divine Mother, Christ, and my angels. I may not see them with my physical eyes, but I can feel and know their presence. I have seen miracles occur when I collaborate and commune with them, and I know this is possible for all humans. I believe that God is not picky. The Divine doesn't choose who they connect to, it is up to us.

We choose. We choose if we want to connect, and if we choose to—well, then the walls fall down and the doors swing open. There is so much goodness and sweetness available for us when we say yes to collaborating with the Divine. And to truly commune takes us way past the day-to-day prayers of memorized scripts.

The definition of communion is: "The sharing or exchanging of intimate thoughts and feelings, especially when they exchange is one of mental or spiritual level." To collaborate with the Divine begins with deep communion—the sharing or exchange of intimate thoughts and feelings with The Divine. This means connecting, talking, asking, and seeking daily. We must learn how to partner with the Divine to move in collaboration and creation.

For me, that is done in my sacred space. My sacred space is a place in my home that I have dedicated to communing with God. It is where I pray, chant, heal, journal, and work with my angels. It is done early in the morning, at a time that my home, which is normally loud and crazy with five kids, becomes quiet and still.

You can find your own sacred space by praying and receiving ideas of where you can place it. I have held my sacred spaces in closets, pantries, front living rooms, and anywhere I can feel tucked away and free to truly connect to the Divine.

To collaborate and commune with the Divine, we must carve out the time. If you want to paint your bedroom, you carve out the time to do so. Having paint buckets and brushes sitting on the floor will never give you the result of a painted room. And so it is with collaborating with the Divine. If you do not take the time to communicate with the Divine, a collaboration will not occur.

As you read through each story in this book, I invite you to create a belief that you too can have these experiences. And that if you set aside time to commune with the Divine in your own way, sacred collaboration will unfold.

You are ready. No matter the path that has led you to this point, no matter the trauma, the old wounds that still ache, the "wrong choices" you feel you have made, or the inadequacy that seems to blare loudly in your ears—no matter what your mind tells you, you are a divine being. It is your birthright to connect, commune, and collaborate with the Divine.

The love that awaits you as open up to receive the Divine in your life is immeasurable. May this book unlatch the golden gates of wonder, miracles, and profound love for you in your life.

Chapter 2

COME PULL UP
A CHAIR WITH US

By: Keira Poulsen

When the inspiration came forward to create this collaboration book, I felt inspired that there would be 22 chapters. I immediately assumed that meant there would be 22 authors.

But that is not what happened. Because that wasn't actually the plan.

I prayed daily that God would bring in the right authors. I sent my angels out each morning to find the women whose stories needed to be in this book. And in six weeks, there were 18 of us. But what about the four extra chapters?

I prayed and saw that there would need to be an introduction and closing chapter. That would create two more chapters, but that still only left me with 20 chapters in this book. As I continued to have the prayer in my heart that two more authors would appear, the time to receive more authors had come to an end, and I was unsure of what to do.

We were on a tight timeline as the publishing date of 2/22/2022 had been spiritually given to me, and the time had run out to find more authors. I was about to submit the final manuscript to be formatted when I was shown who the final author was that would write the other two chapters in the book!

That author is YOU.

Yes, you. I was inspired to ask *you* to pull up a chair and come sit with us in this sacred circle. This book isn't here for you to be a bystander or a witness, but for you to be a voice within it. **A contributor.**

You are here with each one of us. And so, this is your first chapter in this sacred book. You are rolling out the magic that is held within these pages. Thank you for being here with us.

What led you to this book? Was it a friend, a special experience, Divine guidance? Write below how this book landed in your hands.

_____

_____

_____

_____

_____

_____

What does the Divine mean to you in your life?

_____

_____

_____

_____

_____

_____

When you hear "collaborating with the Divine," what comes to your mind?

_____

_____

_____

_____

_____

_____

What does the phrase "commune with the Divine" mean to you?

_____

_____

_____

_____

_____

Are you ready to embark on a deeper journey of collaboration with the Divine?

_____

_____

_____

_____

_____

What has your experience been like with the Divine? Was it strong at first and then forgotten? Has it always been a strong root system in your life? Or have you just recently stepped onto this spiritual path with the Divine? Maybe it doesn't look like any of these situations but instead your own beautiful, sacred story. Share below what that story is:

_____

_____

_____

_____

_____

_____

_____

_____

_____

_____

_____

_____

_____

_____

_____

_____

_____

_____

What are you seeking to strengthen in your own personal relationship with the Divine? How could this relationship get stronger? Is there a desire within you to hear the Divine more or collaborate daily with your spiritual team? I invite you to set an intention as you read this book so that, as you read these women's stories, your desire to know the Divine will be strengthened *and the intention you set here and now will come to fruition.*

If you don't know what you are seeking, then I invite you to pray before you fall asleep at night and ask. There is a magical window of time right before we drift off to sleep where we can send up a request to the Divine. If you send up the request to know what the intention is for you to set as you read this book, and then get up in the morning and take 5-10 minutes to write—the answer will be given to you. Take this opportunity to strengthen your own muscle of spiritual receiving and write below the intention that you are setting as you embark on this sacred experience with us.

_____

_____

_____

_____

_____

_____

_____

_____

_____

_____

_____

_____

Lastly, I invite you to write down the inspiration you receive as you read through each chapter. If you go into each chapter with the desire to receive insight for you and your own life, *you will receive.*

As we read over and over in the ancient scriptural texts: "Ask and you shall receive." These words are the truest words I know.

If you ask, you will receive.

Ask before you read each chapter in this book to receive insight, inspiration, and guidance in your own life. I have created a short journal section at the end of each chapter for you to write down these insights. Writing them down will help you remember them. It will bring them into earthly form and will create them to become real.

The Divine will speak to you if you ask and then receive. These are both action words that will change your life. Begin—or continue—that practice as you read the stories that have been so generously shared within these pages.

Remember that *you are now an author in this book.* Allow that to settle in and become true for you.

Thank you for sitting with us in this sacred circle.

Chapter 3

THE MAGIC PATH
TO OUR NEW HOME
"The Trilogy"
By: CC.elaine

"**T**AKE BOLD STEPS!**"** That was the message God had given to me in a dream one night. It was so profound that the next day it left me feeling shook with a strange sense of trust and empowerment.

The message came to me during a transformative time in my life. You see, I had been living my dream. I was married to my high school sweetheart, we had three beautiful daughters, and I was running my own custom bridal wear business. I thought the prize had been won! But then it came… the shakeup. My whole world got turned upside down. My marriage was over. I lost my business. I was forced to give up my home and my mom passed away unexpectedly during her recovery from a spinal injury. My whole world was falling apart and there was nothing I could do to save it. It was almost as if I was being kicked out of my own life and being thrown onto a path of complete uncertainty. Little did I know, behind the energetic scenes every person, situation, and circumstance was being perfectly positioned for a magical unfolding that I could have never planned or even imagined.

While I was making my way through my transformation and the shakeup that ensued, I held on to the voice in my dream. It was deep and stern, like a direct order from God. It had become my rock, my invisible support, and my guiding light. And it inspired me to formulate a plan for a bold new start.

Now, let me tell you a true story about the magic of the Divine Universe. It's like one giant, magical mystery was unfolding on my behalf. The Universe was literally speaking to me—guiding me. It was sending me signs and clues every step of the way, letting me know that I was safe and that I was indeed on the right path. I was being guided to our new life and to our new home.

So, there I was—a single mother of three with no job, no money, nowhere to live, and a clear message from God to take a bold step. I had been wanting to move back to Atlanta, Georgia, where I lived during college, but the timing had never been right. This was my opportunity to make my move and it was indeed a bold step because I was on my own with three young daughters and no support. I just knew I had been given direct instructions from God. It was up to me to come up with a plan.

Back then, you could always count on snagging a job from a temporary employment agency anytime you needed a quick side hustle. But I needed more than a side hustle—I had to start saving for our big move. The four of us moved in with my brother and the employment agency placed me on an assignment with the Indiana Spine Group making $12 an hour. Keep in mind I had been running a successful bridal wear business for the past 10 years. My assignment was working as the assistant to a woman by the name of Sheetal. We worked for a group of doctors who were conducting experimental spinal surgeries using real surgeries and sham surgeries. They would measure the healing success percentages of the people who actually got the procedures versus those who received the fake procedures. It was a very intriguing study—essentially a study of the placebo effect. I ended up working there for six months and formed a great admiration for my boss, Sheetal. She was of Indian descent, with beautiful, long, thick hair. She was quite stylish and super intelligent. I looked up to her and she took me under her wing, offering me support and encouragement for our big move.

Over the six months I worked there, I was on a fierce hunt for a new home in Atlanta. I even hired a realtor to help us with our search. It was a complex situation for a few reasons. Each of my three daughters were entering their first year of a different level of school. Because they would each be at different schools, I had to find a home in a school district that had A1 ratings for elementary, middle school, and high school. My girls had never been split up because they had previously attended a private school where they'd been together from kindergarten to eighth grade. So that was challenge number one. I also didn't have a new job lined up for when I got to Atlanta, so I couldn't prove any future income. My plan was to make wedding dresses for private clients, which I also didn't have just yet. The next challenge was that my credit was jacked up from months of unemployment and my home being foreclosed. So, you see, I was really banking on a miracle!

It was two weeks before the new school year and we still hadn't found a home. Everyone was turning me down and rent was extremely high for the school district I needed in order to accommodate all three of my girls. Strangely enough, I never felt worried because of my dream. About ten o'clock one evening, I get a text from my realtor, Lisa, about a listing she found on Craigslist that was in our desired school district. I was skeptical, but I looked into it anyway. And, oh my god, it was so cute! It had the exact number of bedrooms I needed and was right at the top of my budget, which was a miracle all by itself. It had a two-sided brick fireplace and a cool loft with a ladder. It felt like a dream come true.

The landlord was having an open house that weekend and I just knew someone was going to get it and take it off of the market. I immediately reached out via text and told them I desperately wanted this home and asked them not to have the open house this weekend. I know they must have thought that I was crazy. He said if I filled out the application and put a deposit down, he would cancel the open house and hold it for me. I told him I would.

Now, mind you no one had seen the house in person, not even my realtor. But I had to act fast or someone else was going to scoop up (my) house. The next day, I submitted my application with my deposit on deck. I get a call from the landlord about my application. He said, "Wow, you're working for a temp agency, your credit is bad, and you don't make three times the amount of rent in income. What do you expect me to do with that?"

I kept my composure and, with the enthusiasm of a naive child, I proceeded to explain what a great human being I was and how I had money saved up and that he could trust me to honor my commitment. (I only had like $2,000) I even went on to say that he could call my boss at the Indiana Spine Group and ask her. I knew she would vouch for me!

The landlord stopped and said, "Wait a minute, did you say the Indiana Spine Group?" I exclaimed, "Yes, I've been working with them for the past six months on a research project and my boss's name is Sheetal."

Now here's the best part. The landlord told me he'd been working on that very same research project as a traveling nerve monitor and had been trying to get a contract with the Indiana Spine Group forever. He then went on to say, "And guess what? My sister's name is also Sheetal."

At that point, we were both blown away. He told me he'd give me a chance, so I sent him my last $2,000 for my deposit, signed the lease sight unseen, and, in two weeks my three daughters, Mr. Nibbles (the guinea pig), and I packed up everything we could possibly fit into my little red jeep and hit the road for Atlanta. After nine hours of driving, we finally arrived to our new home. We had no furniture, no TV, no dishes, or really anything. We only had a couple of bags of clothes, two air mattresses, and a massive guinea pig cage. The landlord, our realtor, and one of my good friends were there to greet us.

The house and neighborhood were perfect! The landlord showed us around and told us all about the home, neighborhood, and property. We even had a fig tree in the yard on the side of the house. That part of the property was owned by the lady on the other side of the fence, but we were welcome to partake of the tree and the land. What was crazy about it is that the tree looked just like a tree that I had put into the "Mind Movie" I created for myself before we moved. (A Mind Movie is like a video version of a vision board.) For the next two years, we called it the Jesus tree.

House 2

Once our two-year lease was up, we were ready to move to a new home, but we needed to stay in the same amazing school district. I was a bit concerned about our next move because the rental rates for the area had doubled. I had managed to land a really great job as a contractor in the custom fitting department at the bridal salon that does the hit TV show *Say Yes to the Dress*. I was earning a pretty decent income but my credit was still on the shaky side.

My girls and I spent every weekend visiting homes and filling out applications to no avail. It got down to the wire and we still didn't have a new home to move into. One day, as I sat in the front window sewing, I noticed a group of neighbors in front of our home pointing to the side yard where our Jesus tree was. It looked like a somewhat heated conversation. I went outside, introduced myself, and asked if there was something I could help them with. One of the ladies introduces herself as the owner of the land on the side of our home where the Jesus tree sits. They were discussing a big landscaping project she was doing in the neighborhood on the other side of the fence. We chatted a bit and I mentioned to her that our lease was about to be up and we still haven't found a home. We exchanged numbers and she told me she would keep an eye out if she hears of anything.

Several weeks went by and we still hadn't secured a new home. I was really starting to feel the pressure because we had already given notice at our current home and a new family was scheduled to move in. One day, as we were backing out of the driveway and headed to the airport for a Cancun vacation for my daughter's sixteenth birthday, I looked out of my rearview mirror and saw someone running up to my car waving a piece of paper. She was yelling, "Hey, hey, Caren!" I stopped and saw that it was the lady who owned the land where our Jesus tree sat. She handed me the piece of paper and proceeded to tell me that a good friend of hers is putting his home up for lease and wants to rent it right away. And it was just over the fence in the neighborhood I live in. I thanked her and told her I would look into it when we returned from our trip.

As soon as we got back, I reached out to her friend, explained the situation, and let him know that his friend had referred me. He seemed just as excited as I was because he had been hoping he wouldn't have to go through the process of putting the house on the market. We were excited because the home was an upgrade from any house we had ever lived in. However, it was also double the rent that I was currently paying. I had never paid so much for rent or even a mortgage before. But I remember feeling in the moment that the whole scenario was a Divine Appointment and somehow an important step along my path, so I trusted it. I referred back to the dream I had two and a half years earlier when God had instructed me to take a bold step. I just knew the divine plan was not yet complete and that this was also a part of it.

The owner of the house immediately, and somewhat naively, approved us for the home simply because his friend had referred me. I really didn't even know this woman and she knew nothing about me except that I lived in the house with the attached side yard that she owned. It was a big, beautiful four-bedroom home in a popular intown subdivision. I guess you could say that I ended up raising my family in that home. We lived there for seven years. Two of my daughters graduated high school and left for college from that home and all three made lifelong friends.

I know what you're probably thinking... seven years! Why didn't you just buy the house? I was a self-employed contractor and was never able to prove enough income in order to qualify for the loan. But it was okay. The house was really nice but also very traditional. And my lifelong desire had always been to experience modern home living.

In the early spring of 2019, the news of the pandemic was just starting to spread. Our final lease term was approaching and, after six years of cultivating a foundation and making lifelong memories, we were about to say goodbye to our family home. The owners of the house were ready to sell. But I wasn't in a position to move. I gave every proposition I could come up with to convince them to let us extend our lease. But there I was, unprepared and on the hunt for a new home.

In my search, we managed to find only one home available in our school district that was at least equal to our current standard of living. We really wanted this house! I went back and forth with the owner for almost a month and, just when I thought we would secure the deal, she decided to go with another applicant. I was done! I was again faced with the task of finding a safe place for my family to live in just two weeks. Meanwhile, day after day, I would sit on the floor in my closet in complete darkness chanting, praying, meditating, visualizing, writing, imagining, working with crystals, talking to God, and calling on every Archangel, Spirit Guide, and Ancestor. I thanked them for divine protection and clear guidance. I was in a space of complete surrender. I remember feeling so strongly that something important was about to go down, but I had no idea what it would be.

And then it happened!

The statewide, then nationwide, then worldwide quarantine was announced. On the floor in the closet I went, I thanked God for this life but asked how I was going to orchestrate such a huge move with all of this chaos going on. Then something clicked. My emotions became neutral and it was like I snapped into a zone. I got laser focused and did everything I could to keep my vibration in a state of joy. I watched puppy videos and funny videos of babies. I hugged and loved on my own babies… we call that the love juice. Whatever it took for me to stay in the vibrational pattern of what I desired.

The next day as I was sitting at my sewing machine, pushing through my projects for the day, I got a text from our current property manager, Chris. He told me the landlord wanted to extend my lease for another year if I was still interested. I sat there with my mouth hanging open, frozen and stunned! Then I fell to my knees and cried like I was in church catching the Holy Ghost. "Thank you, thank you, thank you God, thank you so much. I love you, I love you!" And then I texted Chris back and simply said, "Yes, please!"

We stayed in the home for another year and enjoyed the freedom that quarantine had brought—no deadlines and no expectations. The whole world was on lockdown. As the end of the year approached and I began to focus on our big move, I found myself in an even more challenging predicament than before. I had not worked in a whole year. We were barely scraping by with my unemployment. And in order for someone to let me move into their home, I was going to have to be able to prove that I could afford it. In fact, I needed to show that I was earning three times the amount of rent per month in income. And living in the city of Atlanta, that is not cheap!

I basically ignored that part of the scenario and started looking for homes in the area. Nothing was even on the market. No one was moving because of the pandemic. Everyone in the city was fighting over the two or three homes that were out there because the market was so scarce. And I had nothing to fight with. I had exhausted my savings and was living off of $400 a week in unemployment while rent in our area was over $3,000 a month. But I just knew that somehow, someway a miracle was going to save the day. My motto, for a long time, has been "the path is protected!" I knew, for sure, that I had been walking out my divine purpose. That was the single thing that I was banking on.

Aside from dressmaking, my life's work has been centered around what I call Intuitive Living. It is the practice of tapping into your energetic capabilities and intuition as a daily practice for making the highest moves along your journey. It's about experiencing the magic of life and activating your awareness of Universal guidance and the way Spirit speaks to you using signs and clues that illuminate the way. My history of working with Spirit in this way is deep and my trust at this point is supreme and unwavering! I've come to integrate these practices as a natural way of living in my own life, so much so that I refer to myself as an Intuitive Liver. One of my daughters even has it tattooed on her forearm. I'm painting this picture of Intuitive Living because the next story I'm about to share is truly an experience of Divine Magic.

House 3

Let me start it off with an entry from my journal dated March 6, 2021. We were already one week into March and we had to be out by the end of the month and I still had not found a home. The journal entry was entitled "Our New Home Experience."

Thank you, Divine Spirit, for guiding and protecting me along this journey. Thank you for inspiring me to trust the journey and the way that it is unfolding. Thank you, Spirit, for aligning ALL of the necessary people, money, and circumstances with my heart and my highest desired outcome. Thank you for blocking me at every turn from making choices that are not for my highest good. Thank you that I hear and understand your guidance every step of the way. Thank you that our new home is a beautiful, divine miracle where we feel at ease and at peace. Our new space is stimulating and divine. We all feel so grateful and inspired.

It is the divine fresh start that we all deserve. It has space for each of us comfortably and space for my dress work and Intuitive Living. It is perfect beyond my wildest dreams. And thank you that it is easily affordable for me and brings me grace and peace of mind. Thank you that all of the details are being worked out behind the scenes. Thank you that I have a surge of money coming in to help clear my current rent and utilities as well as paying for the movers and the move overall. Thank you that all is unfolding in divine timing. Thank you that this story and this testimony is going to be of service to others who need to hear this. Thank you that the measure of this challenge of trust is equal to the measure of success on the other side.

I know that I am being divinely guided and I know that my path is protected. My soul cycle is completing and my fresh start is on the horizon. Thank you for miracles and magic. Thank you that I tell this story with so much passion that it inspires so many to step into their divine purpose and live out their dreams. Thank you that we are safe and protected. Thank you that I will know the right new home for us when I see it. Thank you that things will play out so smoothly and miraculously that there will be no question that it is a Divine Appointment. I trust my path and I trust my journey and I trust that my divine purpose is protected... therefore I, too, am protected. I am experiencing divine timing. Thank you that I give my very best to all of the dresses and clients that come my way. Thank you that I exceed their expectations and thank you that I am a Divine Blessing.

Two days later my best friend and my daughter, Zoe, sent me the same listing of a home that had just come on the market two days prior (March 6th). I was at the shop doing fittings when they sent it and wasn't able to really examine it until I got home. Zoe and I looked at it together and we realized it was a part of this cluster of modern homes that we had watched being built around the corner from our current home. I had been admiring these homes for a year. I even said to Zoe a few months prior, "It would be so nice if we could somehow lease one of these homes," but they were for sale only and seemed far out of my price range. But when we both realized the listing was indeed one of those houses and it was for lease in our timeframe AND in our "imaginary" price range, our hearts literally started pounding and racing.

I immediately reached out to the listing agent and asked for a showing for the next day. This was her response to me: *I don't mind showing you the property BUT I just had a showing yesterday with two highly qualified prospects and I'm sure the owner is going to go with one of them.*

For some strange reason, I replied: *If you don't mind, I'd like to at least throw my hat in the ring.* I don't even know what made me say that because I was the least qualified person on the planet at that time.

The next day, Zoe and I went to view the home. Before we went, we said to each other, "If this is *the* home, we will know it because it will have every space that we need." It turned out that it was a three-bedroom house, not four—which we needed since my two older daughters were back home from college taking classes online. We left the viewing quite perplexed because of the way our hearts had been beating and racing the night before. We just knew this was the one. We had a great conversation with the agent during the showing and never mentioned that it wasn't quite a fit. In fact, we enthusiastically thanked her and asked that she keep us posted.

The next day, she called to tell me that the owner decided to go with one of the other "highly qualified" prospects. She said they offered to pay $200 more on the rent per month to assure their position with the home. It really was a modern home with a perfect location and in the best school district in the inner city. I kept my emotions neutral and I thanked her again for all of her help. She even offered to help with my search and look into other listings even though I had already exhausted every other prospect out there. A few days had passed and I had begun looking for homes way out in the suburbs where the schools were really good. I really didn't want to take Zoe away from her friends. It was her first year of high school since the pandemic. But I had to do something because time was running out.

Before I continue the story, I need to mention another dream that I had about a month prior. In the dream, someone held up one of those auctioneer-type paddles with the number 58 on it and showed it to me in the dream. It seemed significant so I wrote about it the next day in my journal. I had no idea what it meant but it felt important.

Now, back to the story. A few days had passed and I get another call from Jackie the realtor. She says, "Hey Caren, the owner decided not to go with the other applicant. She said something came over her and she just didn't have a good feeling and I told her I thought you were the next best candidate!" Mind you, I'm over here with absolutely no money saved and no provable income and a shaky credit score. I told her thanks for letting me know and asked if she could give me a moment to think it through. She agreed but told me not to wait too long because it was a super-hot property.

I hung up the phone in shock! My heart was telling me that this was the home for us. But how in the world was I going to pull this off considering my financial situation? I would need at least $15,000 to cover deposits, movers, and settle up past due rent. It was going to require some real miraculous, divine type magic to make this happen! After I hung up with Jackie, I got the impulse to check my email again. Right away, I noticed that I had one new message in my inbox. Before my call with Jackie, there had been 57 emails in my inbox, and now I had 58. I didn't know what to expect. But the email was from the SBA saying they were approving me for the EIDL loan that I had applied for over a year ago. My loan had originally been denied at least ten times because, somehow, it got entangled with the owner of the bridal salon that I was contracted and they weren't able to figure it out.

But on that day, just after hanging up the phone with Jackie, in email number 58 in my inbox, the loan was approved like nothing had ever happened. Now I had more than enough money to make my move. Again, I was stunned, but also not stunned because I know how Spirit works and I had written the whole thing out on March 6th in my journal.

I called Jackie and told her I was in and asked her what she needed me to do next. She asked for three months' worth of paystubs and a rental history statement from my previous landlord.

I have to be completely honest here. I was seriously trying to think of some way to manipulate my income and paystubs or something because, in my mind, there was no way she would approve me, given my current financial situation. I am generally a very honest person and I believe strongly in cause and effect, but the safety and wellbeing of my family was at stake and, for a brief moment, I was tripping. But then I remembered my own mantra... the path is protected! And the history of the divine miracles that had already happened in my life flashed in my mind. I took a deep breath, crossed all of my fingers and toes, and decided to be completely transparent. I sent her my three months' worth of paystubs from around the same time before the pandemic, along with an explanation stating that this was my usual income and is what I expect to be earning once again when business picks back up. I offered a good faith additional deposit. And her response was... I was approved. I was so floored! My mouth hung open, frozen and stunned. Thank you, God!

But here's the beauty of this story. My birthday is on February 26th, and a couple of weeks prior to that, my aunt who lived in Indiana passed away. She was like a second mother to me and the last of her siblings to die. We were due to move at the end of March and, at this time, I was still unsure of how the way would be made. I had a few new brides I was scheduled to meet with on the weekend of my birthday, but I had to cancel in order to travel to Indiana for my aunt's funeral, which was taking place on my birthday. I remember thinking when I got the news of the funeral arrangements that I couldn't afford to leave just then, and I needed the money for our move. That thought was immediately followed by, "Girl... you are tripping! The path is protected, and you know everything is being worked out behind the scenes. Don't worry, you've done your part!"

After we were settled into our new home, the air conditioning needed a repair and, since it was a brand-new home, it was still under warranty, but they needed the closing date in order to access the warranty. I reached out to the owner for the closing date on the house. The date she gave me was February 26, 2021!

The Universe is always speaking to us, guiding us, and leaving us signs and clues. It is sending us comfort and assurance, letting us know we are on the right path.

What insights, inspiration, and ideas came to you while you read this chapter? Make some notes below:

_____

_____

_____

_____

_____

_____

_____

_____

_____

_____

_____

_____

_____

_____

_____

_____

_____

_____

_____

_____

_____

Chapter 4
CREATING IN COMMUNION WITH THE DIVINE
By: Cami Epperson

Creating with the Divine, for me, is a sacred, holy communion. It is an opportunity to break the bonds of human restriction and allow my soul to fully step forward and collaborate with the Divine Beings and the Divine Energy that guide me in every step of my path. This collaboration opens up the pathway to learning and understanding that runs deeper than any human teaching can offer.

Creating with the Divine requires a Divine connection—a connection to one's own Divine self and the Source who created it. Your Divine self is You—the You that came into this life with a purpose and a plan to execute that purpose while learning along the way. The connection facilitates that learning, and the creation is the execution of the plan.

My belief is that we, each of us individually, knew clearly, before we came to Earth, the gifts we were created with that would be integral in fulfilling our purpose here. Each of us has a purpose. We were not born to take up space, then die. We were meant to make a difference in a way that only we, as our individual selves, can.

Finding that purpose is one of the first steps that comes from the Divine connection that leads to your creations. Connecting to your gifts and understanding what they are meant to be used for opens a world of possibilities that will change your life and the lives of those around you, even if it's in small, almost unnoticeable ways.

I came into this life feeling displaced. I felt I did not belong here on this Earth, and I longed to return to the place from whence I came. I spent a lot of years feeling the heaviness of the burden of this life—its mundane tasks and the seemingly pointless motions I was going through simply because it was a part of mortality. I was gifted the ability to feel a Divine connection from the beginning, but a lot of times it only made me long to return all the more. I was biding my time until the day I could return to the glorious place I dreamt of, the loving arms of my Creators, and to "really begin my work."

As I got older, married, experienced trauma, married again and then had children, I got so lost in the physical effort my day-to-day responsibilities required of me, I was exhausted. I didn't always know I was exhausted, but life had taken its toll. I felt I had just about lost my connection, though not entirely. I had moments where I felt close to it, but they were fleeting. I honestly didn't know who I was anymore, or what I was meant to do beyond washing dishes and cleaning up toys. I knew I was fulfilling the desire I had for as long as I could remember—to be a mother—but in the middle of it all, I felt little joy. I was not the mother I dreamed I would be or that I wanted to be.

I was frustrated and felt there was something more, but I wasn't able to put my finger on what it was. But I knew that I had to find the connection that would remain and not disappear once a moment had passed. I would catch glimpses in moments of prayer, study, or teaching, that were powerful enough to leave me wanting more. It was the feeling of a deeper, more constant connection to the Divine that brought so much peace and energy at the same time.

There was a night in the spring of 2019 when I felt the longing for that connection deeper than I had ever felt it before. Maybe it was a culmination of the years spent grasping at straws and I finally gave in. I had avoided asking for it, asking for signs or experiences, because in moments past when I had hoped that I would feel something, typically it would not be what I was looking for and I was left disappointed. This night—this moment of pleading with the Divine for a connection to the other side, to something Divine, a real connection I could feel-- would begin a series of events that would change my life in ways I could have never anticipated.

I didn't have a monumental experience that night and, once again, I was left disappointed in the moment. However, I didn't realize it then, but looking back on it now, I see that it was the beginning of a shift that would lead me into an awakening and a path to deep Divine connection and creation. It opened a door, by simply asking, that allowed the unseen to meet me in this physical world because I was ready to receive it. I knew it was there, and I wanted it more than just about anything.

Within just a couple of months, my world was turned upside down. My family moved, and, while in limbo between homes, I fell into a deep depression that brought me to my knees, in more ways than one, and on more than one occasion. It made me so deeply and wholly reliant on God because I had nowhere else to turn. In another moment of pleading, I asked that it be lifted so that I could begin to function again in life in general, and more specifically as a wife and mother. I saw clearly the ways in which I was completely not okay, and how it was hurting my family. I saw the places in my life that needed to change in order for me to step into my Divine roles more fully. My soul was ready to embark on a journey of discovery and healing to prepare me for the work that lay ahead.

Over the next several months, people fell into my life that completely directed that healing. My world broke, in the best of ways. It was painful and beautiful at the same time, and absolutely necessary for the growth that needed to happen. I compare it to hiking up a steep mountain. The climb can be exhausting. The ground may crumble below your feet. But you will have moments when you can stop and rest, take in the beauty of the views in front of you, look back to see how far you've come, and regain your energy to continue on. You know the destination will be even more breathtaking that what you see now, so it will be worth every bit of hard work and exhaustion that you experience along the way. You just have to keep going.

My beautiful views on this mountain that allowed me to rest, rejuvenate, and renew my energy were several deeply spiritual experiences with the Divine Mother. I could never accurately describe these experiences in human words, but they absolutely fulfilled my request and my pleading prayer to feel a deep connection to the other side. This connection would become so absolutely vital in my creation process and purpose that it needed to be unbreakably strong. It needed to be obvious. It needed to be 100% undeniable.

Almost a year into this journey, I felt I needed to start a new Instagram account, specifically for the purpose of telling my story. I didn't know why, but the feeling was unrelenting. On Mother's Day in 2020, we were visiting some family for the holiday weekend. Around 5 am that morning, I was woken up with an energy and feeling that this was the day. I quietly climbed out of bed and sat on the floor in an upstairs bedroom. With my husband still asleep on the bed and my youngest asleep on the floor next to me, I typed out 2 posts that would begin pouring out my heart—unashamed and unrestrained—to the world. Or, I felt, at least as much of the world that needed to read them. Two hours later, with my heart beating out of my chest, completely trusting the Divine direction I was being given, I hit the button to "Post." And then I waited, and watched the response.

Within two days I had several messages thanking me for these posts and relating their own stories. They were people wanting to talk, to know they were not alone in their struggles. It was then I knew that there was something that needed to be heard, and so began the opening up of the gift of writing. Though, again, I didn't realize what would come of it at the time. I simply felt like I was telling my story and sharing what I was experiencing. I didn't fully understand the purpose behind it, but I knew it was being led by the connection I had found with the Divine around me, and the Divine within me.

Just over a year after my crash course in Divine connection began, I stood in awe as I watched my pathway unfold. I distinctly felt that all of it was happening now, at this time, for a specific purpose. There was something I needed to do with this gift I had been given… but I didn't know what exactly. I didn't even know where to begin looking for the knowledge of what I was to do with it. Again, I asked, and the door was opened.

I was on Instagram one day and saw a post from my husband's cousin, and I don't even recall what it was about. All I remember is seeing the tag "@keirapoulsen" lit up like a neon sign and the clear voice within me saying, "Contact her. Now." So, I followed the tag and messaged her to set up a time to talk. After our first conversation, I was all in—I just needed to get comfortable with investing in myself. It's something I had never really done, nor been comfortable asking for, and yet, it was necessary in the process. I couldn't shake the feeling, despite all of the excuses I could come up with not to and the fact that her whole premise at the time was becoming an entrepreneur (which is one thing I never had any desire to be), that Keira would be the one to show me what to do with this gift.

And she did. It took about 2 months of more guided healing to clear the space for the creations to come forward, but once they did, it was like the floodgates opened. The Divine saw that I was ready and willing, that I sacrificed and invested in myself and Them, and They were eager to send inspiration.

My first creation within this new space was a sketch, which sparked the unmistakably clear guidance to write a book based on this sketch. In fact, the sketch would inspire the cover of the book to be titled, "Conversations with the Divine Mother: Finding a Personal Relationship with Divinity." I never planned to be an author. I never even considered it. My mother is an author, not me. Yet, here I was, being faced with sharing my newfound connection with the Divine Mother, in a book that anyone in the world could read. It was scary to be that vulnerable.

I had gotten to the point where I could share my past, or a current insight, in an Instagram post, but to share something so deeply sacred was a little terrifying. However, I had been so clearly instructed and led the whole way, so I drew strength and comfort from feeling deeply that there were people out there who needed it. I could almost see their faces. I trusted the Divine guidance and left the outcome in Their hands. It would be exactly as They it needed to be. Nothing less. Those who did need it would find it, for They would bring them to it.

I have since discovered that this is how I work in my creations with the Divine. I feel the guidance, I see the vision and purpose of it, I trust, surrender the outcome, then get to work. I may get scared, have voices inside and out tell me all the reasons I shouldn't, but I have learned to decipher those voices from the calm, peaceful, and empowering ones of the Divine. I have also learned that, scary as it might be to take the leap, there is always, always, always something better than I could possibly imagine or create by myself on the other side of following Divine guidance.

Divine guidance also always has a way of pushing me beyond my comfort zone. Once I received the Divine instruction to write this book in the middle of October 2020, I was intuitively given a date on which it was to be published—Christmas Day 2020. That was eight weeks away. Eight weeks to write an entire book and have it published. As a busy working mom of three kids, I knew I wouldn't have time during the day to dedicate to this book. I promised the Divine Mother, as I felt clearly that She and I would be collaborating on this book, that I would show up every morning at 6 am for 2 hours, until I had to get my kids up and ready for school and dedicate that time to Her and our writing. I even felt guided on the weekend of Halloween to take the time to get away for a couple days to receive and write.

I showed up each morning, as promised, and opened my heart and mind to Divine receiving. I would pray that the messages that needed to be shared would come through me. I had questions that I would ask, and She answered in a way that I could understand and feel deeply of Her love. I spent these mornings in Holy communion with the Mother who I came to know and love on a level that I have never before experienced. It changed me more deeply than I knew was possible.

Four weeks. I remember vividly the morning it was finished. I wrote the final words and felt the finality of it. Four weeks from the day I started, with exactly four weeks left for editing and publishing. That morning I was both celebrating and mourning. I was celebrating the accomplishment of bringing forth this book in Divine time, and through Divine power, and yet mourning the fact that my time of deep collaboration with the Divine Mother, feeling Her so present as She sat next to me every single morning, was now over.

As the details of publication were ironed out, I had the very distinct knowledge that this was only the beginning. I knew on a soul level that this book was the gateway to even deeper connection, even bigger creations, even more ways to help others who seek it, and there was no reason to mourn. A Mother as loving as the One I felt would not use me and leave me, She only wanted to strengthen the bond further. She only wanted to encourage and empower me in my gifts and purpose to bring me to new heights.

This Divine love I felt, and came to be so familiar with, has been the catalyst and central purpose in all I have done since then, and all I will continue to do. Divine love is unlike anything human, though there are relationships that may come close. It is everlasting, ever-enduring, ever-present, wholly accepting, holds no bounds, and requires nothing. The term "unconditional love" was always one that I never truly understood, until now.

Because I have felt this love so deeply, I have a clear understanding of my role in sharing it and providing the opportunity for others to feel it, as well as helping them find their own place in Divine creation, in whatever way I can. Creation is this work that will dispel the darkness that looms and surrounds us. It is through the love of the Divine that we will each find what it is that we are meant to bring into this world, what messages we are to share, the people we are meant to reach and the means by which to do it all.

When we are sharing through this Divine Love and Divine Power, we are also led to the people who are doing the same. There is strength in numbers and we need that support as we embark on such a monumental work that is meant to bring the Light that will heal souls and heal the world.

As each person is ignited in this love, as they feel their worth and purpose—truly feel it so deeply within themselves that they can't deny it—as they know they are loved for ALL that they are, that the dark *and* the light each serve a purpose, and that they have an important role to play in this world, a Light within them begins to glimmer.

As that Light glimmers and this one person believes in the Divine voice within that whispers confirmation of their Divinity and the guidance of each next step, whether they believe yet that they can make a difference in this world or not, they know that the Divine sees something in them that they cannot see in themselves, yet. All it takes is trust, surrender, and action.

A Light begins to spread through the earth with each footstep they take on their own path in creating with the Divine. Each footstep is a point of contact where a creation of whatever sort—a message, an act of service, a kind thought shared, a work of art, the written word, a song sung, or a musical masterpiece—has been given a place in humanity. In whatever form the creation may take, it places upon the earth a Light that continues to spread, like a growing pool along the ground, long after their foot has left its point of contact. One step after the next, with one creation after another.

Each creation has a Light and Life of its own that allows the work of the Divine to continue. We, as mortal humans, have a vital role in this work. It could not be done without us. It is our gift from Them to be given such an opportunity. As we take this opportunity to fulfill that role, our lives are fulfilled and enriched infinitely in ways we could never conjure on our own.

As much as the plague of darkness seeks to take over the earth and all of humanity, we have greater power in spreading Light. With each step of each person who works in communion with the Divine to bring forth the pieces that are theirs to bring, the pools of light continue to grow until they have each spread far enough to connect with all of the other steps, all of the pools, to create one big pool of Light.

None of us should feel, as I sometimes do, that the Divine expects us to heal the world and restore the Light to its fullness all on our own. It was never meant to be that way. That's why we have each other. All of our work—all of our creations—are interconnected. They complement each other as we serve the same purpose in bringing the Divine into the view of our human experience, while allowing Their Light and Love to touch the hearts of those who will accept Them. Our individual Lights merge as they grow, creating a single, connected, Divine Light that covers the entire Earth, within which darkness has no power.

We will always experience opposition, but darkness will not have the power to overtake us as we remain engaged in the work of Divine Creation. We were made for this. We were created by, and from, Divinity. As such, we hold within us that power to also create, through that same Divinity, the works that carry the messages which will heal our hearts, our souls, and our humanity.

I sit in prayer and meditation almost every day, asking what it is that I need to do next in my own work. As I receive ideas and inspiration, I am also given a clear vision of those who are waiting for the messages of Love that can, and will, come through as I continue to take the steps I am guided to take, by Divine direction, to spread my own pools of Light. Sometimes the work lies within myself, my own family, my own circle. Sometimes it reaches far beyond. In all circumstances, the work is equally important and vital to the lives it will touch—no matter how small or far-reaching.

The work involved in creating with the Divine, as well as the outcome we experience, will never be what we expect. One thing I have learned is that not only do we create to serve our fellow man, but we also benefit personally within the level of healing and learning we gain from the experience of bringing forward a creation that has been completely Divinely guided.

Sometimes it's scary to step into this new space of creation and expand in our Divine purpose. However, it is completely worth mustering every bit of courage it takes. Creating with the Divine is one of the most exhilarating rides I have ever been on. Everything that comes with each rise and fall of it never ceases to amaze me. I would have never dreamed of learning or experiencing everything that I have. I have learned how to quickly dispel the darkness that used to cripple me as I discovered details about myself, the purpose of my life experiences, and how they integrate with my Divine role. I have experienced the intricacies of the healing power of the purely unconditional Love of the Divine. It is an education that I don't believe I would have been able to gain otherwise, or in any other way. I have found joy and purpose in my own role as a wife and mother that I was previously missing. All of these experiences, and more, continue to flow as I regularly seek my purpose-driven, holy communion with the Divine, feel the guidance in my creations and see the vision of them, trust, surrender the outcome, then get to work.

What insights, inspiration, and ideas came to you while you read this chapter? Make some notes below:

_____

_____

_____

_____

_____

_____

_____

_____

_____

_____

_____

_____

_____

_____

_____

_____

_____

_____

_____

_____

_____

_____

_____

Chapter 5

CONSIDER THE LILIES
OF THE FIELD
A LESSON FROM GOD ON ABUNDANCE

By: Angel Lyn, MSW, Soul Mentor

"I'm too poor to pay attention." That's what my father said when I was growing up. It was his way of making a joke out of a subject that was the source of great stress for him—money.

He was a quiet man, honest, hardworking, and full of integrity. He was raised on a ranch in Nevada and had many skills that lent themselves to physical labor jobs. For most of my upbringing, he worked as a heavy equipment operator in excavation. My parents had six kids—four girls, then two boys. I am the 4th child. The advantage of being a middle child is perspective. Being sandwiched between the older siblings and the younger ones meant I was able to see the stresses, strains, and worries that each child brought to our parents. I determined at a young age to please my parents and not be a source of concern for them. My siblings are truly golden individuals. As far as character goes, my five siblings are stellar; yet, parents inevitably worry, and mine were no different. My parents did not expect anything outrageous of us, yet it was obvious that my dad wished he could help prepare us to be financially successful adults.

"You're smart. Go to college and get a good job." This was always my dad's advice to me. I knew education was important to him. Neither he nor my mom had gone to college, and they also struggled with finances. Beyond available income, they had a lack of financial education. Conversations around money were rare and tense. I knew my dad wanted something different for me. From the time I was in elementary school, my dad paid me to get good grades. I got $5 for every "A" I earned on my semester's report cards. I loved his reaction each time I showed him my grades. I felt like he was proud of me.

I knew my dad saw me as smart. And being smart was a good thing! It meant money was in my future. In elementary school, I talked about being a lawyer or the President of the United States. I set high goals for myself and I was sure they were possible. I told him once when I was very young, "I can do anything I set my mind to." He grinned and nodded in agreement. That was our pact. I was going to make him proud. I would be successful. In everything I did, I wanted to hear his famous three words: "Ya did good!"

My parents were also actively religious. I was raised in a Christian church, commonly referred to as the "Mormon" church (The Church of Jesus Christ of Latter-Day Saints). In this religious culture, a woman's place is in the home. I was taught that being a stay-at-home mom was a righteous choice and I interpreted that to mean that any family with a working father and a mom who was able to stay home was a family doing it "right." Many church lessons and frequently quoted phrases of church leaders reflected this position, such as, "No other success can compensate for failure in the home." I did not realize that, one day, these two aspects of my upbringing— my father's desire for me to be educated and financially successful, and my church's teachings that a woman's place is in the home—

would collide. Based on my interpretation of my own religious beliefs, I could not seek a profitable career AND be a righteous wife and mother at the same time. It was one or the other.

I went to college as my dad (and mom) had hoped. I thrived in college. I received scholarships and had top grades. Academia was a setting where I excelled: reading, comprehension, thinking critically, writing, presenting, and testing are all areas that come easily to me. I completed a Bachelor of Social Work degree and was greatly inspired by the research and work experience of several of my female professors in that field. I began to consider pursuing a Doctorate of Philosophy from Oxford University in Social Policy. And then I got engaged.

I remember one of my female professors asking me what my post-graduate plans were. I told her, "I'm getting married." She paused and said, "And? What else? What are you going to do next with your education?" I was slightly stunned because she was a professor at a university owned by the LDS church. I figured she knew what the "routine" was for most women—you get married, you have kids, you stay at home. She said to me, "Angel, yes, it is a given that God wants you to get married, have a family, and raise them righteously, but He also has a mission for you! He can use your gifts and talents to build the kingdom in many other ways." I felt like she believed in me. This was not just a general pep talk. I felt she truly believed that I could succeed. I thought about her words and my future. My fiancé was already enrolled in a graduate program, so I decided to apply to the same university and I was admitted. I was married just before my program started and, two years later, I completed a Master of Social Work degree and had birthed my first child just months prior to my graduation.

Check, check, check. I was on track! I was doing what I had been taught were the right things to do: go to college, get married, and start a family. Now it was time to stay home. That is what I felt like I wanted at the time so that is what I chose. I proceeded to have a total of five sons in under nine years. We moved several times and struggled financially while living on one income and squishing into one- or two-bedroom apartments for most of our marriage. I watched, feeling confused and lost, while friends our age bought their own homes, took family vacations, and drove nice vehicles. It seemed like they had enough money to not only cover the basics, but well beyond that too! We did not.

In addition to our education, we were also totally dedicated to our religion, or so I thought. We dedicated ourselves to practicing the religious routines of the Mormon church. My husband and I constantly had church assignments in leadership positions. Among other titles, my husband served as the "Branch President" for several years, which is the head clergyman for one of our congregations. I was taught to look to my husband for spiritual guidance and trust in his leadership. We went to church weekly and I followed the at-home routines of daily prayers, scripture study, and family devotionals with our children. Despite dedicating ourselves to all the *right* things, I felt like my husband and I were disconnected from each other. It felt like we were failing God somewhere and I wondered why we were not worthy of the blessings of financial success. There I was, reliving the financial patterns of my parents—we never had enough money. There were many tense conversations around finances and this put a strain on our marriage. I sought counseling, we met with a financial advisor, and I tried hard to do all the *right* things. Yet nothing improved. We were emotionally distant and disconnected for the majority of our marriage, behaving like roommates who co-parented. Outwardly, we portrayed a "happy and perfect little family." Inwardly, I was dying. Emotionally, I felt completely alone in my worries about our finances and our inability to truly communicate. He did not seem concerned at all. I felt frustrated with him. I felt helpless and hopeless. And eventually, those feelings began to manifest themselves physically.

After having my 5th child, I suffered from deep depression, stage 2 adrenal fatigue, Hashimoto's, chronically elevated cortisol levels, and I was pre-diabetic. I was so physically and mentally exhausted that I felt like a horrible, failing parent. I felt like I had given all of myself to my family, but we were struggling financially and I was unhappy. I did not know what else I could do to help our family. I periodically thought about going to work. I believed I was more than capable of earning a substantial income. But the thought of putting our kids in childcare evoked so much guilt and shame, as if it would be a disappointment to God, that I could not force myself to do it. I also had a lot of resentment toward my husband; I felt like I was keeping *my* religiously-assigned role of being a stay-at-home mother and I wished he could just do *his* role and be the financial provider.

Just after our 14th wedding anniversary, our marriage began to unravel. I discovered some very serious and illegal financial dealings in my husband's life. The circumstances were shocking. I could not believe that the person I was married to (and lived a very religious life with) had been lying to me and many others for years. My reality shattered. I immediately turned to God in a way I never had before—directly!

Although I had been taught to pray my entire life, I realized something crucial amidst this crisis: I had trusted everyone else's definitions of God. I had prayed to God according to the way others had instructed me to approach Him. I always used a 4-step pattern with my prayers because I had been taught that was the proper way to pray. I believed God was a "Him" because that's what others had told me. I was constantly reading and studying words from the leaders of my church, and the words of prophets from past eras, to configure my understanding of God. I just wanted to know God and follow Him, so I had trusted in everything I was told. In this season of my life, I realized that everything I thought I knew about God and everything I practiced was after the manner of a mortal template.

When I discovered my husband's hidden actions, I felt shocked and betrayed. I felt like I could not trust mortals with anything any longer. I was done looking to humans to tell me how to navigate my life. "Look where it has gotten me!" I thought. "I am exhausted and unhappy. I have been lied to and I am totally alone."

My belief in God was hanging by a thread at this moment, too. "If everything else in my life is fake, I wouldn't be surprised to discover that God is fake, too!" I was experiencing an existential crisis. I was questioning the meaning of life itself. With no guarantees, no presumptions, and absolutely no preconceived expectations, I walked into my bedroom and I talked directly to God in a bold, new, and candid way. And I got answers! Immediate answers! They came as clear thoughts, simple to understand, yet not always emotionally easy to follow. The answers that came in that moment, and every day since, have consistently contradicted mortal ideas, past beliefs, and commonly held cultural norms. I remember feeling that the answers that came from that first, direct conversation seemed so far from my own logic that I figured they had to be coming from a source outside of myself. "Maybe it is *the Source*," I had thought. "Why not trust these thoughts as Divine answers? I don't have anyone else I trust right now! So, what do I have to lose?" Everything in my life pivoted from this point forward, as I practiced the simple pattern of asking, receiving, trusting, and acting.

One powerful point of recognition is that I noticed my ego was very quick to want to reject the immediate answers that came from my questions to God because they did not seem "logical." The answers did not align with the mortal programming and conditioning of my mind, so they were easy to want to reject. The Spirit showed me that rejection was the exact opposite of receiving. The more I practiced candid conversations with God, receiving the immediate, clear thoughts as answers and acting on those answers with courage, the more I noticed, and could count on, the persistent presence of my mind's temptation to pull me into a rejecting and dismissive pattern. I began to intentionally choose to suspend any attachment to fear and practiced noticing the dismissive and rejecting thoughts. I then utilized them as evidence that the direct opposite was the truth I was looking for. In this manner, I was able to overturn my past habit of perpetually rejecting answers to my prayers! I replaced rejecting answers with receiving answers.

I heard this phrase from one of my mentors: "The depth to which I breathe is the depth to which I can receive." This mantra became a reminder to take deep breaths as I am conversing with the Divine. Deep breathing helps me with the process of receiving. The act of inhaling supports taking in and assimilating the Divine's answers. The process of exhaling represents escorting fear and doubt from my physical body. Receiving answers from God required me to begin to trust myself and trust that I was capable of communicating directly with my Creator—the Divine Source of truth, light, and love. It was through this practice that I noticed I had been systematically conditioned to not trust my inner voice, which is my soul! Society, culture, religious influences, and even education are all among the authoritative voices that taught me to look to, listen, and trust voices outside of myself, instead of my own inner voice.

Trusting myself felt radical and new to me. I had to source courage in order to act on the Divine answers. I reminded myself daily, "Trust yourself and the answers. Have courage and take action." These words brought on new meaning to the word "faith." This new way of conversing with the Divine illuminated a startling pattern from years prior: I had, unknowingly, frequently rejected and dismissed the answers to my prayers because they came fast, did not agree with logic, and required me to trust myself. My ego mind had been in charge back then and it had fought adamantly against these elements.

In a four-month time span, after beginning to speak directly to God, being open to receiving answers, and acting on those answers fearlessly, I received spiritual direction to separate from my spouse and prepare for a divorce. My husband said, "God would *never* tell you to do such a thing!"

"Well, that's what *my* ego mind said too!" I thought. However, this process of conversing with God had never been clearer in my life and I no longer needed anyone else to agree. I proceeded to follow the directions I was receiving from the Divine.

In my religious culture's perspective, I was facing a monumental failure. Our "forever family" was not going to last. But when I looked at my options, the fear around that cultural "failure" simply faded. Life became very simple: either I follow Divine guidance or I choose to follow the source of fear. I became clear in my awareness of the presence of two inner "minds." I have a fear-based mind (I believe this is my ego), who always wants to maintain its reputation and seeks approval, acceptance, belonging, and love from other humans. I also have a love-based mind, which I call my soul. The soul only cares what God thinks of it. The answers that came through my soul's mind always brought with them a presence of this liberating pattern: light, truth, love, joy, peace, and freedom. No fear. None. I didn't even worry about my reputation. Listening to my soul's mind always led me to mind-expanding experiences, heart-opening emotions, and personality-enhancing changes. I refer to these moments as "HOLY SHIFTS!"

For months, I operated under the pattern of asking, receiving, trusting, and acting. I separated from my husband and closed our family business. But now I was faced with a new reality: I was 39 years old and had been a stay-at-home mom for 14 years. I had five sons and was going to be divorced, so I needed to provide for myself and my family. I collected lists of job openings, beginning with those in the field of social work. I sent emails to companies, I began to draft a resume, and I had my first phone interview with a potential employer. The weight of my future sat heavily on my chest. I noticed doubt encroaching on my mind, body, and heart. But then I paused. I realized that I was going through the motions of what I *thought* I was supposed to do to get a job, but I had not directly asked God what I should do about income.

I spread my notes and job applications out on a table. I took a deep breath and cleared my mind. I submitted myself to one desire— to do the will of God. And then I said, "God, here are some opportunities I have found for work. I am wondering what to do to provide for my sons?" Once again, as with all of the recent questions I had posed to God, there was an immediate thought response: "Consider the lilies of the field." That was it. It was clear, it was recognizable, and it was accompanied with total peace. "What does it mean for me?" I wondered. I knew the phrase was a reference from the Bible, but I was more familiar with it as lyrics from a musical number I had performed many years earlier with my church choir. I began to search online for the exact Bible passage, hoping to gain a context for those words and explore their meaning and application for my life.

Luke 12:27-32

27 Consider the lilies how they grow: they toil not, they spin not; and yet I say unto you, that Solomon in all his glory was not arrayed like one of these.

28 If then God so clothe the grass, which is today in the field, and tomorrow is cast into the oven; how much more *will he clothe* you, O ye of little faith?

29 And seek not ye what ye shall eat, or what ye shall drink, neither be ye of doubtful mind.

30 For all these things do the nations of the world seek after: and your Father knoweth that ye have need of these things.

31 ¶ *a*But rather seek ye the kingdom of God; and *c*all these things shall be added unto you.

32 Fear not, little flock; for it is your Father's good pleasure to give you the kingdom.

My two "minds" wrestled with each other over this passage. "The message is clear," said my soul's mind. "But not logical," said my ego's mind. "The message is spiritual." "But not mortal." "The message is peaceful." "But not probable." The soul and ego went back and forth. I knew which mind was which. I had a choice to make... which "mind" should I trust? I quickly concurred with my soul's mind. I had been in full trust of my soul's mind, adhering to the answers I had been receiving from God, for a solid 9 months, so despite the ego mind's programming, which attempted to lead me down the path of fear, I chose to let go of the question of how I would financially provide for myself. The scripture passage seemed to speak to me that the Creator of all things had a plan in place to provide for all the needs of its creations. "The lilies don't cry to the sky asking when it's going to rain." I thought. "They don't stress over the quality of the soil, nor the hours of daylight sun. They just ARE." Although knowing how to operate as a human by these ideals was not clear, I recognized that it was God's business to deliver the "how" and it was my business to simply trust. I felt more and more peace as I committed to embrace and trust these words.

A week or so later, an elderly friend of mine (who knew I was separated from my husband) asked me, "What are you doing for work now?"

"I'm open and looking," I replied.

"Well, I could use some help with cleaning my home," she said, "Would you be willing to do that?" My soul resounded with, "This is a YES!" So, I agreed.

We set up appointments for the month and I began to visit her consistently. This woman shared with another elderly couple in her neighborhood that she had hired a cleaning lady, and that couple reached out to me and hired me as well. Within just a few months, I had enough cleaning jobs, paying $25-30 an hour, to cover my basic expenses and I still had quite a bit of time at home with my boys. Cleaning for senior citizens was a gift beyond anything I could have imagined! I was able to schedule my cleaning appointments around my boys' needs and whenever I had any scheduling conflict, like a sick child, I was able to simply call my clients and reschedule their cleaning appointments. My clients were so gentle, understanding, kind, gracious, and supportive of me. They loved hearing stories and seeing pictures of my boys every time I arrived at their homes. I felt enveloped in love! It was like my children suddenly had multiple sets of grandparents.

Also, it was relatively easy work. Their homes were so clean! I just needed to clean their bathrooms and kitchens, do a little dusting, some vacuuming, and occasionally I was asked to help with other simple tasks around their houses. While cleaning, I spent most of my time listening to audiobooks about consciousness and spirituality. I received so many personal, life-shifting, timely insights from these inspirational materials. This path provided me not only with income, but with the time and resources I needed to heal as I transitioned through a separation and divorce. I thanked God repeatedly for how perfect this option was and felt amazed that it was not something I had ever even considered!

Once in a while, pending expenses would exceed my income. I would catch myself thinking, "***How*** am I going to pay for this?" I began to notice this thought came with accompanying fear and doubt. The word "how" carries inherent doubt and fear. So why was I beginning a question for my Creator with such a doubtful and fearful word?

"How ludicrous!" I thought. "Am I doubting God?" I felt humbled by this awareness. I was learning through my audiobook studies that fear was the antithesis of love and truth. Attaching to fear led me away from God. When fearful thoughts around finances appeared, I would intentionally shift gears away from fear to love. I would repeat in my mind, "Consider the lilies of the field," take a deep breath, and then tell myself something along the lines of, "I know in whom I have trusted. God, I apologize for attaching to fear and I release it. You have taken care of me in every moment of my life, and I know you've got me in this moment too." I practiced repenting of fear and anchoring to trust. And God worked out the "how" every time.

Each time I had an experience where fear surfaced around finances, I felt the belief in scarcity surface too. They were my father's fears and beliefs. I also felt my own fears, frustrations, and resentments from my past marriage. With conscious awareness and intention, I was able to recognize the presence of these things and choose to not attach to those beliefs, thoughts, and feelings. Instead, I chose to redirect myself and align with truth: God is in charge. God has made all resources and they are abundant and sufficient for man. God loves me. I love God. I am worthy of all that God has created for me. I choose to receive. I trust the processes of life.

And then I would simply carry on with my life, trusting that truth always leads to freedom. Financial resources continued to show up at unexpected times and in unforeseen circumstances. I monitored my ego mind and sought to stay open to receiving the financial blessings, rather than reject them. This sounds so easy, but I assure you, it is not. I invite you to look at yourself and ask the question,

"When and where am I rejecting things in my life?" Here are a few areas to investigate to enhance your awareness:

1. When given a compliment, how do you respond inside your head? "YES! I AM THAT!" Or, "They're just being nice. If they really knew…" Do you receive the compliment or reject it internally?

2. When offered help at the grocery store, do you say, "Sure, you can take my cart to the car!" Or do you say, "No, I've got it. Thanks." Receive or reject?

3. When your spouse offers you love, such as, "I love you! You are so beautiful! You are an amazing partner!" Do you receive it or reject it? "No, I'm not! I've put on weight. I'm not doing enough at home. I'm always behind on things."

During this period of my evolution, I discovered that I rejected so many things in my life, such as those listed in the examples above. I rejected things unconsciously, out of conditioning and habit. I discovered I harbored mental fallacies perpetuated in my culture, such as, "It is better to give than receive." I had been programmed by these types of phrases to feel guilty for receiving and to believe I was more holy or righteous if I were the giver and not the receiver! The Spirit said to me, "Angel, if you struggle to receive a compliment from a mere mortal, how do you think you're doing at receiving all that I have to offer you?" Mic drop, Jesus!

Believing these lies and practicing the habit of rejecting were keeping me from receiving the abundance of God, including the abundant love of God! I had been living in a manner that was trying to climb a "stairway to heaven" (I also call it my "Modern-Day Tower of Babel," if you are familiar with the reference from Genesis 11:3-4). I had been trying to earn my way into heaven and prove my worth and value by my deeds, completing all the checkboxes of religious rituals and practices, while simultaneously rejecting the love of God. I was so entrenched in my habit of rejecting love that I had to make a conscious effort to begin receiving. Practicing the skill of receiving was like taking a muscle in atrophy to the gym daily. With consistent effort, I strengthened that spiritual muscle.

Guess what else was revealed through this process? I discovered that my financial status was always in direct alignment with the energy of rejecting or receiving that I was emitting into the world! When I was attached to fearful thoughts and rejecting, I was in scarcity; when I was attached to love-based thoughts and receiving, I was in abundance. Money is just one form that flows either away from us or towards us on the currents of fear and love. Relationships, connection, health, opportunities… these, too, flow to us or away from us, depending upon whether we are fearfully-living and rejecting them or lovingly-living and receiving them.

The lesson from God to "consider the lilies of the field" ushered in a dramatic shift in my life. I recognized that I had been relying heavily on myself to make things happen and not adhering to Proverbs 3:5-6 which says, "Trust in the Lord with all thine heart; and lean not unto thine own understanding. In all thy ways acknowledge him and he shall direct thy paths." Once this scripture really hit home and I began to live it, I recalibrated my manner of being and practiced the skill of receiving. I now see receiving as the master key that opens the floodgate of abundance.

Since the time of my divorce, I have passed on all of my cleaning jobs to another single mom who was ready to receive and heal. I now enjoy a life of splitting time between living in southern Utah and Hawaii. I coach individual clients, host women and men's groups, host retreats for women and couples, and have an epic relationship with the love of my life. I revel every day in the awe, wonder, and majesty of God. It is amazing the things that can happen in our lives when we learn to truly speak and listen to God.

What insights, inspiration, and ideas came to you while you read this chapter? Make some notes below:

Chapter 6

RUNAWAY TRAIN

By: Katie Jo Finai

The medical team surrounded me, jamming one end of a hose through my nostril and down my throat. It was just a dime-sized, clear, hollow tube, but the pain and humiliation were incredible. I knew the hose was breaking the membrane behind my face as I squirmed and hacked. The device snaked its way down my throat despite how hard I protested.

I felt the hands of doctors and nurses tying me down with forceful derision. Their glares were stronger than the fluorescent lights pulsing above my drugged eyes with an unforgiving strength. That godforsaken tube began to vacuum pump all the bile from my stomach.

It was clear that these professionals could be saving *other* lives instead of dealing with someone like me. Plenty of patients in this emergency room were hurt, maimed, or fighting for their lives. If I strained my neck, I could just make out the lobby a few feet away, full of deserving people. But I was a nuisance. I was someone who was making others wait. Even through my hazy awareness, I heard the side conversations in clipped tones.

"Privileged...young...girl."

"Teenage princess...wasting their time."

But, as is the case with overdoses, time is of the essence. I knew that they wanted to get the drugs out of my system before the toxins were absorbed into my bloodstream. Once my stomach was fully pumped, I gagged further when the snot-covered tube was extracted. Trails of mucus fell onto my long-sleeved, baggy t-shirt. My bare legs writhed in discomfort as they filled my stomach with charcoal to absorb any poison that the pump missed.

Blinking fresh tears out of my eyes, I dared to glance to the side of the room. My father stood there in silence. Arms folded across his chest. Still wearing his work dress shirt and slacks. Rage and terror were written on his face as the medical staff saved my life.

I was eighteen.

Once I was considered stable, I was unceremoniously transferred to the psych ward with other female patients. In this musty, shameful area of the hospital, I was officially classified with the other "mentally ill" individuals.

In the corridor where they confined me, there was another teen. She was anorexic, but I noticed there were a lot of people here from diverse backgrounds. Surprisingly, most of them were middle-aged and married, all highly religious. Two days after I had been admitted, a psych tech took pity on me and gave me some medical scrubs to wear instead of the soiled t-shirt I was still in. I tossed the t-shirt into the waste bin with my underwear. I wiggled my toes in the luxury of fuzzy blue socks with plastic treads. It was much better than being barefoot.

At night, all the doors were automatically locked and red lights blared from the ceilings. In the morning, I saw smears of dried blood on the recreation room floor that the cleaning people had missed. Rumors eventually reached my ears, and I learned that a mother of six, with a missionary son out in the field, had tried to use the aluminum foil box teeth to slit her wrists.

The testing was relentless. Days were filled with paperwork, questionnaires, psychiatry interviews, group therapy, and pills that came in small, clear plastic cups on the blue tray of hospital food. Then more tests... more tests... and more tests.

Because I was bulimic, my calorie intake was carefully monitored. I was accompanied by a tech on restroom breaks, who listened as I counted loudly, "One, two, three, four, five," as long as I was out of their sight.

As a few days went by, I tried to imagine that the hospital ward was like an indoor summer camp. We played cards, billiards, ping pong, and social masking games like in polite society. Every one of us pretended to be something we weren't. I did my best to pretend I had it all together, holding up a facade and finding a "clique" while working out the pecking order.

But in the quiet of night, it wasn't just my own demons that came haunting; I could hear the demons of other patients. The silence was broken sporadically by the quiet whimpering of pillow-smothered crying.

That psych ward was a small-scale version of the outside world. Our lives were dictated by authority figures telling us how to think, speak, and act appropriately. We were told what being happy was and were handed pills to numb any other ideas.

As a young adult, I saw the medical staff as my jailers, perpetuating the same reality I felt so lost in. I was a lost voice in the wind. My cries of warning that the system was broken were answered by the system saying, "It's not us. It's you."

Seventy-two hours is a standard timeframe to be held in a suicide ward.

I was there for ten days.

The staff was trying to prove I was mentally incompetent. Everyone else got visitors, but I was on restriction. Technically, I was an adult, but my parents were able to claim authority and conspire with the staff of therapists to protect me from the poor influence of my friends. Because I stuttered and paused when I spoke, their theory was that I had lower brain capacity. The incessant testing had to prove there was something wrong with me. It couldn't possibly be the pressures of growing up in a society whose suicide rate was the highest in the nation. It couldn't possibly be the constant pressure of perfection smothering me like a sleeping bag as I was shoved into the trunk of life's expectations.

My test results were identical to a beautiful blonde woman in her forties, who I noticed was stuck in that place as long as I was. Apparently, girls like us were anomalies. At home, she had two children and an affluent husband. That was the problem.

On paper, we shouldn't be there. According to our life stories and circumstances, everything was fine. The analysis said we were emotionally and mentally healthy adults. According to their testing outlines, it didn't make sense for us to attempt suicide.

Yet it wasn't accidental. It was a clear choice.

I was so tired of holding up the image of being okay; navigating the battlefield of teen girl pettiness and the pressures of being the perfect daughter, friend, and student. It was exhausting to weed through the boys who wanted to date me with ulterior motives. They wanted my body but not my soul.

I couldn't walk on eggshells around the cool girls anymore or spend more time wondering why my last boyfriend didn't want me. I had been a go-to-church-every-Sunday and read-my-scriptures kind of girl who had lost her virginity to him. Because I thought he was worth it.

Only now, under the ideals of my pious upbringing, I felt that I was worthless and no one would ever want me. After all, *he* didn't want me anymore.

On top of that, I was also tired of trying to be skinny. I was so tired of taking 90-120 diet pills and laxatives every few days because my body tolerance levels had become so high. I couldn't afford that many pills, and had been shoplifting them for months now. So that day, in the middle of spring, I decided to overdose. Burdened by the guilt of having eaten too much dinner and the fear of getting fat, I tiptoed to the family medicine cabinet and grabbed every pain medicine bottle I could find. I knew that if I took enough, I would die or get my stomach pumped. In both circumstances, I could stop worrying about getting fat from eating too much dinner.

I had scribbled "I'm sorry" onto the yellow notepad next to my bed, taken off my jeans, and crawled under the covers. My mom found me later with the pill bottles and the note. My dad had frantically driven me to the hospital while she stayed home with my five siblings.

The psychology tests eventually came back negative.

Katie Jo wasn't mentally handicapped after all.

They learned that my brain moved so fast that my mouth couldn't keep up. Periodically, I had to backtrack, circling around to give language the opportunity to catch up. What looked like mental slowness was actually the opposite.

When the head psychiatrist read my results to me, I sat perched upon a white vinyl bench in her consultation room. My gaze seared into her, hating every word she said and that fake wig she used to cover her gray hair.

I had been held prisoner, under the premise of my stupidity, and now, with the scores and evaluations in, they could not legally keep me another day. I stood with defiant triumph, returning to my hospital bunk to pack my belongings. I was full of so much anger that I couldn't see anything except the crisscross bars on the windows and the locked doors. Why couldn't they see that the world was broken? Wanting to leave the system, to break out of the craziness called society, was the most natural thing anyone could want.

I think, not long after that, I would have tried to commit suicide again. And that time, maybe I would have succeeded, except Misha showed up at my parent's house a few days after I got home from the psych ward.

From the sanctuary of my bedroom, I noticed Misha had left her car running in the driveway. The sound of her voice trickled down to my room as she spoke to my parents at the front door. Misha was older than me, and had graduated from college. I knew she was an elementary school teacher and married to an accountant. She was also my ex-boyfriend's big sister. We had been close friends throughout the relationship. While she was *his* sister, she felt like the big sister I wished I had.

Cautiously, I crept up the stairs and peeked around the hallway corner. Misha saw me and said: "I came to ask you to live with us. Get what you can carry."

Without a word, I returned to my basement bedroom, grabbed a duffel bag of clothes, and climbed out the window and into Misha's car. Opting not to leave through the front door was decidedly my best bet, or I'd have to pass by my mother's face of perpetual disappointment.

For the next six months, Misha left a note on my door every morning before she left for work. They said things like "I believe in you" or told me about the greatness that she saw in me. She and her husband didn't really talk to me or try to fix me or figure me out. And, while I was there, I created art.

I kept cardboard inserts from empty boxes at the restaurant where I worked. After late shifts, I sat alone in their empty parking lot and smoked one Swisher Sweets cigar before heading back to Misha's house to stay up till morning, sketching and coloring with Bic pens and Crayola colored pencils.

With cheap acrylic paint and brushes, I painted on every surface I could, including the closet doors in the bedroom where I slept. Push pins filled the walls, and Misha and her husband graciously didn't chastise me for the damage.

I surrounded myself with wild pictures, dreams, and meaningless, senseless, poorly done, haphazard art. It was a way that I could process the energy around me. I finally found a way to take the chaos inside of me and put it somewhere else. I could draw, sketch, and create color and vibrance and magic. It was perfect and imperfect.

During this journey of healing, no words came to mind, nor thoughts or solutions. It was like a drug or a river that I could simply ride, flowing with the energy that swirled around me.

It was a lifetime of drawing pretty flowers in vases that broke open. Inside I found the ugly, the real, the clashing colors, the whimsical creatures, and the blood red emotions I didn't know how to process. I was just an eighteen-year-old girl who didn't know what it meant to be a woman or lover or anything else.

Those six months broke the dam inside of me, letting loose the Katie Jo who had been told she wasn't enough, wasn't doing it right, couldn't do it, or didn't matter. It was a wailing echo to the sky that had been buried beneath good manners and crossing my ankles when I wore dresses.

I was in the grocery store a few blocks from Misha's house when I bumped into a neighbor of the beautiful blonde woman in the hospital whose test results matched mine. The neighbor had visited her in the hospital and recognized me. That blonde woman had died. A month after she was released, her son found her hanging in their garage.

As passionate and cleansing as the art was, I still didn't care whether I lived or died. I didn't feel like there was anywhere I truly belonged.

At the restaurant where I waited tables, I nodded pleasantly and filled coffee cups. I listened to people complain about their eggs or steak being cooked incorrectly as I pocketed dollar bills and lousy tips with placid neutrality and plastic smiles. I began paying off my mountain-sized hospital bill one dollar at a time.

I often walked to work to save gas money. To get there, I saved time by crossing through a railroad yard—it shaved a mile off the trek. This dilapidated part of town wasn't well trafficked or maintained, and I often crossed through a broken barbed wire fence.

One hot afternoon, the path through the railroad yard was blocked by a moving freight train. The splashes of graffiti passed like frantic flash cards in front of me. I stood in my work uniform, perplexed. For a year, I had cut through this path without ever seeing a train pass by. It wasn't common.

I knew that the detour around the railroad yard and over the viaduct bridge would add significant time to my journey, though I'd be lying to say I was concerned about being to work on time.

Looking left and right, there was no end to the train in sight. I had no idea how long I would be waiting. The grunting rumble of the locomotive taunted me. The train was giant—boxes and cars jumbling, iron squealing as gummy machinery oil and rusty scents pickled in my nostrils. The heat of the afternoon sun reflected off the ground, combined with the friction from the railroad tracks, and it permeated the air around me.

I kept still, stoically observing the barrier in my path. My ponytail was limp, sweat blistering across my brow.

Then, suddenly, I exploded into an Olympian sprint toward the moving train. The thought of *"I bet I could catch that"* had barely touched my mind like a lilting feather before I was off.

I didn't second-guess or check my surroundings for witnesses. Within a few feet of her metal tentacles, I veered hard to the right to race parallel with her. I heard the crunch of the gravel under my sneakers as I pumped my legs furiously, managing to match the speed of the train.

Sucking in fast breaths, I darted glances at the churning wheels, trying to guess the correct distance to jump so I wouldn't be dragged beneath the train. I reached out my left hand to the boxcar ladder and, with sheer stupidity, I jumped.

The gritty ladder rung held true in my grasp—my damp palm clinging powdery metal. I swept my legs up to the deck between cars. Somehow, I made it.

In the space between the cars, the thrum of the traveling train vibrated through my body. I knew that the train would soon be in a more populated part of town. Briefly peering around the side of the train car to gauge my target, I took another chance and leapt once more. For a few heartbeats, I was a flying squirrel, airborne—before I hit the dirt and rolled haphazardly away from the track.

The landing was shocking and painful. My elbows were scuffed and light road rash decorated my palms, but otherwise my dusty uniform was the only evidence of what had just happened.

Rising to my feet, I hurried out of the rail yard and through the barbed wire fence before someone noticed me. When I found the sidewalk, a smile crept onto my face, even as the adrenaline wore off and my scrapes throbbed with every heartbeat. I was alive. No one had seen me jump onto or off of a moving train. But I had done it.

It was careless and stupid, but I was alive.

That night, when I found myself back on the edge of my borrowed mattress, I reflected on my suicide attempt. I felt like a speck of dust in a world of dirt. Questions began circling over me like vultures.

"Who am I? Why does my life matter? What do I bring that no one else has brought before? I could live and die, and nothing in this world would be different for my having lived in it."

Hopelessness ricocheted off the surface of my skull before I happened to glance up at one of the sketches pinned on the wall. It was a cartoon-ish portrait of a woman's face. Her hair was orange and yellow and red, bold and free with wafting curls. Her face was kind. She didn't smile, but her aquamarine eyes were gentle.

When I looked at the image that I had created, my heart lifted.

Seeing the whimsical drawing and tenderness in the expression of the face that stared back at me brought some peace. My art was creating a distraction. It made me momentarily forget about the pain and confusion I was in.

"Well, there's that," someone seemed to say.

I understood the meaning. If I had died, that picture wouldn't exist. It may never grace the walls of a museum, but when I looked at it, it brightened the world a little and "there was that."

A spark of life ignited somewhere inside of me that day; it said that I mattered.

I didn't have to do grandiose things and save the world. Small things mattered too. The world would never make sense, and perhaps the toughness of life never would, either. Our inner and outer turmoil could bear down on us so heavily that simple things seemed like monumental obstacles, but amidst the heaviness and rage and resentment that were often there, I could choose to be part of the solution.

Glimpsing that brief truth didn't fix everything in that moment, but it started the sliver of light that I began to feed throughout my life. I was still a girl working at a bad chain restaurant and I didn't know where my life was going, but now I knew that I could make it through. With a little risk and a little light and creativity, I would be okay.

Whatever the world thought I should do, whatever blockade stood in my path, I would make my own rules. Maybe I was broken or maybe it was the world. Maybe, I guessed, it was both of us. Or neither.

The crossroads between being a child and adult was just the beginning of my rollercoaster life. I decided to embrace the highs and lows. Life is risk and pain and barriers. It's freight trains blocking your path, but it is also kindness, and daring to take the risk to jump.

All of this, encased in one big, beautiful, messy work of art, is what it means to create with the Divine. I knew it wasn't time to let the spark inside of me die. I was going to be authentically myself. I was going to courageously follow my heart. I was going to break out of what society said I should be or how I should feel. And I knew I'd do it all with kindness because others around me were hurting too.

From that moment on, I made a commitment to create with the Divine, that I would make sure my actions ignite my soul beyond time and expectation. It became as simple as being in the moment and having the faith to meet it—to meet *me*.

For me, that process meant art, drumming, dancing, writing, sunrises and sunsets, seeing joy in my child's eyes, and holding the hand of a friend in laughter or tears.

Divinity isn't outside any of us. It's not an outward journey that others can validate; it's the path within. Divinity isn't something you find. You realize you *are* it. You feel it and know it when you are being true to yourself.

Ask yourself: what do you do that you lose hours in? What can you do for eons of time and still feel invigorated and inspired? What gives you inner peace?

We aren't here to save the world, be famous, or be different. We aren't here to have it all. We are here to contribute in our own way.

In a sky full of darkness, we are each one star in the pocket of the universe, like billions of others. But our little lights still matter and our little lights may be enough to guide another traveler's way.

Creating with the Divine is in the silence and the noise. It's the color and the bland. It's the abyss and the trail, the mountains and valleys. It's all around us and it's hidden.

Divine is undefinable.

So are you. So am I.

Be it.

What insights, inspiration, and ideas came to you while you read this chapter? Make some notes below:

_____

_____

_____

_____

_____

_____

_____

_____

_____

_____

_____

_____

_____

_____

_____

_____

_____

_____

_____

_____

_____

_____

Chapter 7

CONNECTING WITH THE DIVINE THROUGH MOVEMENT

By: Kerri Alicia Galea Price

As a soulful fitness instructor for almost 15 years, I know the power of movement in the body. I have seen it work through myself and others, whether we're lifting weights, sweating in cardio, or doing yoga.

When I was asked how I create and connect with the Divine, the first word that came to my mind—without hesitation—was movement. Then my ego started to take over and said, "Um no, how can we connect and commune with the Divine though movement?" But then I heard my first thought again and was really loud! *Movement.*

Often, people think communing with the Divine can only take place when we are in meditation or prayer, but this puts the Divine in a box, and the Divine definitely doesn't live or work in a box.

The first time I became aware that movement was much more than simply exercising was when I found myself wallowed up in grief, trauma, and loss from the loss of both of my parents and my twin brother—all to addiction. My twin's death, specifically, made me experience the dark night of the soul, and my world went dark. I lost myself with his death. Nothing really changed on the outside, but on the inside—everything changed. On the surface, everything "looked" good and was the same, but under the surface, everything was numb.. I was dealing with the trauma of growing up in addiction, my experiences of losing my parents, and all the baggage that comes with grief, plus trying to raise emotionally healthy little ones at the same time.

I had always exercised because I felt like it was what I should do. I am a fitness instructor, after all. But I also love working out. I loved teaching and connecting with people through movement, but I never connected it to my relationship with God and my spirituality until my soul needed to experience movement more fully. It was then that I started experiencing God more while moving my body. What shifted? What took place in my heart that made me unpack what moving my body really meant and how it could serve me better?

I remember specifically when God told me, "You have the tools—now expand them. Delight in your movement as a dialogue with the One who created you physically and spiritually." Our bodies have been incredibly constructed by God. The muscles, tissues, ligaments, organs, bones, receptors, cells, think about how divine this truly is - the miracle of your body and how it moves. It is perfectly made, and made to move.

We spend so much time with our body, but what about spending time *within* our body to truly connect to our purpose and to God? This came full circle for me. Logically, we think of exercise, fitness, working out, and moving our bodies as ways to physically lose weight, stay healthy, and have longevity. These are all true, but I got curious about what else is true for this tool that God has given us. When I started connecting more emotionally and spiritually to the way I moved my body, there were big changes that happened.

I have been a holistic health coach for years and have always focused on physical health. I always knew emotional and spiritual health were necessary. However, the idea that physical health and spiritual health were a twin flame became so loud that I could not ignore the burning in my soul. It wasn't just about going through the motions anymore, it was about feeling them and embodying the partnership of this new revelation. I could hear God's voice more. I felt empowered, and therefore God could create more *through me* because I was now in alignment with what body movement truly meant. I started to understand why God wants us to move our bodies. There were days where I could not find the words but I found that when I, or others, didn't understand the feelings, the best way to express was through movement.

I found that moving my body was the only real way to cope with my emotions. There are times when I have not felt capable of moving forward from tragedy and trauma, but the mere act of exercising moved me. I started connecting with my body and God. I started praying in new ways during my workouts. I found joy in the Divine again. I became more determined, motivated, engaged, and present— not only physically, but spiritually. God gave me a soul, and my body is the home for my soul. So, taking care of my body also meant taking care of my soul.

If I ever thought that I could care about one and not the other (and worse, if I thought God cared about one and not the other), I knew I was fooling myself. I felt a call to be a steward over my spiritual self as well as my physical self because I know these are both gifts from God and are deeply connected. I believe that if you want to get serious about your spiritual health, you can't ignore your physical and emotional health.

Our bodies change both physiologically and psychologically when we work out, and no matter how broken-hearted, paralyzed, or devastated we are, our biochemistry shifts because we're moving physically. Our brain chemistry changes and endorphins release—making us happier when we move our bodies. Exercise also creates a change in our state of being and gets us in a flow with our bodies. This powerful combination of endorphins and state change give us temporary relief from pain and sadness.

What a beautiful thing, right? It's a recovery for our body and soul. We're all recovering from some experience or circumstances. Movement is essential. I never thought this habit of working out would help me spiritually and emotionally, but just like healing, movement is not linear.

Take note of your posture, polarity, personal space, and how you interact with others. Really hold the space and ask yourself, "How does my body need to move today to heal?"

I have found that the more in tune I am, the more my movement changed. My movement became congruent with my words and what I was feeling. When your body and mind are in harmony, there's consistency between what you say or feel and what you do. Movement is a simple—yet layered and complex—medium of communication, not only with yourself, but with the Divine. Let's explore this together.

What other words mean "to create?" What words mean "to commune?"

The words create and commune are verbs, which indicates an action. And action equals movement!

Movement is medicine. Movement moves us though life. Movement breeds freedom. Movement is a gift from the Divine. Movement is energy. Our body is our soul's home, and the house of our soul craves and needs movement to thrive. We are fire, water, air, and spirit, and none of these things sit still. Fire, water, air, and spirit are not tame. We are action; we are movement. We are not meant to be stagnant.

A beautiful way to create and commune with the Divine is through authentic and intentional movement. When we are in motion, we have the power to move energy that is unwanted and does not serve us. We can use motion to move energy that is not ours, but we've taken on from the world, or motion to move energy that is unconsciously allowed in our body.

We all have a purpose, a place, and a movement. God gave us dominion over our bodies. We have control and ownership of this holy gift. Many people call it a "mind and body connection," however I believe it is the opposite—the body and mind connection. Why? Because the body is the vessel for the soul and heart, which connect us to the Divine. The body is also the vessel for our brain, which connects us to logic, learning, and knowledge. The body helps us have a deeper connection with our soul and heart. The body leads with movement. We are not simply humans, we are human beings, and being is another verb. Movement is an act of being, doing, then having. Most of the world believes the opposite. Having, doing, then being. But this is not how the Divine works. He works in the energy of *being,* which is through movement.

The body is a multi-dimensional vehicle with a divine source of light woven in every cell, atom, and electron in our body. The body is the spirit manifested into form. When we develop a deeper understanding of how we can move our bodies and the role it plays in spiritual growth, we discover that the body is the ultimate messenger of the Divine. Movement forces us into having the conversations with ourselves and with God that society is afraid of having. It helps us express our experiences with nonverbal expression, moving emotions up and out. It allows us to truly embody things on a soulful level. Where is the safest place God could have placed tender, vulnerable, and fragile organs, muscles, tissue, and cells? They can't live outside our bodies. The masterpiece of it all flowing and moving together perfectly creates our body. Within the coding of our body is the divine design of the innate intelligence for creating, moving, and growing. It is the most magnificent, intricate container of the life inside us—the most healing place known on this planet.

Do you realize the power of your body? Do you realize the power of movement? And do you see that its power to heal, nourish, and give life begins or ends with movement? Your body is an appendage of your heart, your creation, and the divine light you hold. Movement is a mind, body, and soul expression. We can promote and unlock the freedom of the expression that we are sometimes afraid to unleash. But movement in our body creates movement in our life. Movement changes our vibration. Movement can change our state of being.

There has been research exploring body-based movement approaches for mental and emotional health treatments. Intentional energetic movement therapy provides a way to express oneself, but also offers a path toward healing trauma and lifelong strategies for managing stress. When we are healing, we hear and see the world how God truly wants us to, instead of through the lens of our deep wounds.

At the end of the day, you can change the shape of your body all you want, but living inside of it won't be pretty. It's time to close your eyes and go inside yourself. Don't just be with your body, be *within* your body. The body you're looking for isn't out there—it's in you, and we can captivate it by with movement. Do you realize that the greatest spiritual practices involve movement? Our ancient ancestors had movement practices to increase their spirituality. What did they do to call upon their messengers, angelic realms, and healers? They moved; they danced. Don't you think we can also use this as a spiritual tool to call upon our light leaders, assigned teachers, and guides?

Movement is an energy exchange, not only with the world but with the Divine. Movement creates a transcendence within our body. It's like nectar for our soul. Your blood pumping, sweat dripping, heavy breathing... the most spiritual downloads I have gotten is when I am moving my body. Whatever you're going through—the heartache, the stress, the frustration, or longing for more fun, more play, more everything... we can always return home to our body because that is where things can be released and freed. Moving our bodies reminds us to let go of perfection and get back to our body's most natural form: expression. It's there that we can be ourselves. The body is the technology of bliss. Understanding that will help you to discern boundaries, connect to the internal motivation for self-care, and lead a life based on the pursuit of joy.

When I hear people say that they can't move, do yoga, dance, or lift, I know it's not true. You can. We can all dance, we can all move, we can all sing, we can all create. The "I can't" comes from the belief that our value lies in our perfect execution. Movement is a primal form of expression and there is no "right way." You just need to find a way to express who you are inside. There is an unspeakable beauty in loving being in and with our body. Self-value is transmitted to all that surrounds us. Every time we choose to move, it is an opportunity for us to drop into the body and touch the joy waiting to move you. Bodily movement is a cue for your brain to wake up. Movement signals to the brain that there are decisions to make, opportunities to take, and pleasures to pursue. Movement signals to the brain that it's time to come out and play!

I love the concept of showing up as your favorite self. Not best self, better self, or higher self... just your favorite. I feel like movement allows for this grace of just being your favorite. What does it look like to hold space with movement as your favorite self? What does it feel like?

Often, we start to pass self-judgement when we move our body. We become rigid and strict and only move out of obligation or fear. Somewhere along the way, movement becomes a shadow. Sit still, stay here, don't move, behave yourself, stop doing that. You feel you need to prove your worth first. And, just like that, we stop moving subconsciously, which then turns to feeling unsure about it and being self-conscious.

However, if we can show up to exercise as our favorite self—the game changes. This is something very few of us spend time being. This leaves room for grace and helps us recover from being perfectionists and people pleasers. We can lose ourself in motherhood and life, and I truly believe one way we can find our favorite self again is through movement.

There is a saying that "passion without precision is chaos." The Divine gave us our sacred bodies out of chaos, and we get to create with precision. We move with the Divine as a co-creator. We are Divine by nature, greatness by design. Our body receives connection through the Divine so, if our body is designed to move, then moving it will certainly help us tap into the divine gifts, light, and love that it offers. We are not meant to be stagnant humans. We are not meant to be idle. Sacred, intentional, and authentic movement connects us not only to divinity in general, but to the divine feminine and our Heavenly Mother.

When we don't move, we lose energy. We become stiff and immovable. We stop listening to our body and our souls. When we choose not to move, dysfunction happens, and when we become dysfunctional physically, it affects us emotionally and spiritually. Everything that is temporal is also spiritual and everything spiritual is temporal. That's how our Creator works in full circle and synergy. We need to move physically to move spiritually.

I call this voltage. Yes, we all know endorphins peak, but these molecules also act on your endocannabinoid system. This is the same system that's affected by tetrahydrocannabinol (THC)—the active compound in cannabis.

Like endorphins, exercise releases endocannabinoids into the bloodstream. You know that rush you feel over your body? The tingling, the high-on-life feelings? That is your body's nervous system responding and releasing the "feel good" chemicals. Your body does this automatically; it's like natural moving medicine. But it only happens when we choose to move our bodies. This system is already there waiting to send the electric voltage of soulfulness through your body to channel with the Divine. How amazing!

The greatest purpose of our lives is to love the Divine. But how do we express love if we can't physically see or touch the Divine? Each of us has a body, and when we choose to move our bodies, it provides a tangible way for us to know, love, and create with God. We are made to move in God's direction, by God's initiative, and at God's pace. Our bodies will speak to us if we listen. Our bodies will teach us as long as we're moving through heart, soul, mind, strength, energy, and stretch, using movement that engages the body and its senses, as well as the mind, including the imagination. When you move daily, you discover the masterpiece the Divine has created in your life.

Our body speaks in rhythms (movement), governing the beats of our hearts, the expansion and contraction of our breath, the waves of our digestion, and the sleep and wake cycles. It is no surprise the divine created the autonomic functions of the nervous system to respond while we are moving. Regularly offering your body safe, rhythm, repetitive sensations and movements helps us shift to a more regulated state of being. When we are regulated and in homeostasis, we are no longer in flight or fight, but balanced. A blanched body and nervous system unlock the secrets of the divine.

The most sacred and amazing spiritual transformation begins with a physical transformation. We can't transform if we don't move.

If we don't move, then we become complacent in our body, mind, and soul. The human heart needs to be attended to by intentional movement and rituals. When we practice finding our rhythm, it lessens anger, sadness, and stress, thus letting creativity flow and connect to the Divine.

This power of moving your body is waiting for you to claim it. Take up space for yourself. Claim your health, soul, mind, and body.

Authentic movement is building something inside of you that you cannot lose and that no one can take from you. Play out loud and let your symphony take shape through movement. Also, let's remember that, usually, moving our bodies is coupled with music. Our body responds to rhythmic beat, because that is how our hearts pump.

Think about babies for a moment. In the first year of life, how much movement does a baby do? They are developing their fine-motor skills, learning body parts—simply discovering their body and how to move it. Remember when you were a child and you lived wild and free? You didn't have a care in the world. As a baby, you moved your body before you could ever talk or walk. Why? Because your body is your language; a moving message. Movement is fun! It's playful. It reaches to our inner child and heals our wounds. It is a beautiful masterpiece helping emotions to be moved through, up, and out. And when emotions move through us, we become healed, and we can hear God's voice in our lives.

I always say that moving is like story-telling with your body. What story can you write while working out? What are parts of your story that need healing? How can you grow, evolve, and expand? Some of my greatest spiritual connections have come at the gym because I learned to tap into God while exercising. I know this might sound crazy, but stay with me.

Why has our modern culture evolved to ignore, or even deny, that during physical movement, a positive energy is created? This movement creates self-healing energy. Why does our modern culture look at this as just a "weight loss" tool—an external thing—instead of a spiritual tool and an internal thing? We currently live in a disembodied world. We disconnect our body from our soul and mind. You cannot do anything separate from your body. Nothing happens without movement. I'll say that again—nothing happens without movement. This is how essential it is to life on a soul level. Letting your body move without apologies helps us create liberty within ourselves, which creates vulnerability. When our spirit becomes vulnerable and contrite, the Divine can speak to us. Creating this for yourself creates safety and magic. It's all about experiencing something while we move. You can use your body to manipulate speed, momentum, and connection from head to toe. It is seriously so cool to watch as you move the divine creation of your body and see what it can truly do.

Unlike plants and trees, we are not tethered by roots. We are not left to wait for the world to come to us. Rather, we can go into the world to step, walk, run, dance, and move. When is the last time you paused to ponder the wonder of your body? Not just its uniqueness and elegance, but the fact that humans have them at all. We are living, breathing, speaking, working, moving images of the Divine himself, going out to a created world to display The glory. The Divine thought it was best that we not be fixed to the ground, but human beings that could move around and fill the whole earth. Pretty awesome, right? It is truly about trusting your body's innate intelligence (that was given to us by the Divine Creator). As you trust, you're going to feel a deeper comfort manifesting in your body. You'll feel energized. It will feed and ignite an awakening on so many levels in areas that you even didn't see as being connected. Everything is so interconnected spiritually that we don't see it physically while we are working out.

However, once you become conscious and aware of this connection, beautiful things happen as you are moving your body.

There are so many options to move our bodies. I believe in three different ways to connect with our bodies—not only physically but spiritually. When we can create synergy with both, a magic happens with the Divine. I invite you to bring your body out of exile and into a deeper dialogue with me.

When we move our bodies, we move energy that does not belong. When we clear out that gunk, the Divine can better speak to us. Feelings are just energy in motion. Tap into these three energies to commune and create with the Divine when you exercise: **power, energy, and balance.**

When I say power, I mean strength training. The energies and emotions of power are masculine, fierce, strong, resilient, undaunted, and sometimes angry or frustrated. For energy, I am talking about cardio. These energies and emotions are happiness, love, playfulness, fun, agility, force, vibrance, sexiness, and freedom. Balance is for active mobility and recovery. The energies and emotions of balance are feminine, tranquil, compassionate, soft, steadfast, light, calm, and clarity.

Our body is like a pendulum, and if the pendulum swings too far one way, it will swing back the other way even harder, meaning your workouts might not be serving your body or your soul. We have become a society that is all about "the more you do" when, in reality, it's about creating synergy with what, how, and why you move your body. I have realized that after experiencing hardship, the "grind and then grind some more" mindset can actually cause more trauma, which will make you feel more disconnected from the Divine.

So, I reinvented and birthed my holistic trifold framework to move your body. And it works! I created intentional workouts, dialed in physically, emotionally, and spiritually. I healed my life, health, body, and soul externally through the movement of my body while staying in tune with what was happening internally as I worked out. There is no better self-healing energy than when one participates and creates in movement with the body in order to connect with God. The body actually needs all three energies to feel in homeostasis with movement. Too much of one thing gets the body out of balance. We need to experience these full range of emotions and spiritual feelings! Our body is beautiful, our body speaks, and our body keeps the tally of our soul. The next time you do a work out, how can you make it intentional instead of just going through the motions? What's the *why* behind it?

As a group fitness instructor for almost 15 years, I found my passion through liberating women through inspiration mixed with intentional, powerful movement. I encourage all of you to look inward and listen to what your soul is craving. When was the last time you truly let go of all your insecurities, fear, and inhibitions and just let your body move the way you innately felt like moving? Maybe childhood? Maybe college—after you had a shot of tequila?

We were all born with the instincts to move our bodies. You already have all of the things you need to be successful with your fitness health. There is no shiny unicorn here. When music comes on, our impulse is to want to move, but a lot of us let fear take over, and let caring about what others think steal our joy. Don't let them. When you turn on your favorite song and let your body move however it wants, you will witness magic. See where the music and movement take you. Oh, the places it's taken me!

When you exercise, what is mostly activated? Your breath and your heart. Breathe, and then breathe again. Feel your heart beating. As we partner with our body, we change our energy and start to see, hear, and feel things differently. Our perspective changes, and when your perspective changes, you start to have new ideas for actions you can take to create movement in your life. You have so many systems supporting you that go beyond the physical to keep you balanced.

It's not about a moment; it's a movement. Mindful movement is the power the Divine gave you over your body, mind, and soul. A rapid heart rate, flushed face, blood pumping, endorphins, quick breathing, and any other physiological responses peak when we are exercising. We also know that a single emotion can last about 90 seconds. Think about how many emotions we can work through when we are moving our bodies!

Move for just 90 seconds and witness the emotion you are feeling without thinking about why the emotion is there or judging it. Observe it without identifying it, then move through it. When we are working out, this practice becomes more effortless because we are already in motion. This helps us work toward a regulated nervous system that can hold capacity for our feelings and emotions. The more we practice being with our body and its sensations, with or without an emotional charge, the greater we grow our capacity to really witness the Divine. Moving your body is an investment of your soul.

This is what moving your body truly means—to feel good in your own skin. It's a holistic approach to awakening your true self, connecting and communing with the Divine, and healing through hardship and grief. When you move, you summon the courage to let it all go. Take it all in. It's just you against you—no competition, no comparison. Just you moving your demons out.

Intentional and authentic movement tends to lead to powerful outcomes and amazing insights, realizations, and results. Once we heal, we can become a beacon of light and a leader of our body to co-create with the Divine and open up a spiritual gateway.

Now that we have learned so much about movement, let's apply this in a practical way. Remember that you can't mess this up. There are no expectations, only intentions. Before you work out, ask the Divine to show up and help serve you. Maybe you are working on something specific. I tune in to my body first—check in and just really listen to it. I usually match how I am feeling to the workout I choose to do.

Do you need to release anger? Okay, let's take that anger to a dumbbell. Maybe we need a punching bag or something to push. You need this anger gone, so acknowledge your feelings, and then slam down the medicine ball or pick up some weights. You will start to feel strong and you will feel the anger leave your body.

Are you tired? Does your body need to rest? Okay, let's find some solace in stretching and breathing, moving our body slower in yoga. Maybe you need to open up your heart to receive something from God, so you ask before you begin your workout. You do a heart opener pose and just breathe, focusing on your intention to receive from the Divine.

Are you craving energy? Do you need to allow yourself to tap into the divine feminine? Do you want to be childlike and playful? Move your hips, shake your booty, sweat and have fun! Try dance cardio, leap into a really fast-pasted HIIT workout, or go for a run. Say a prayer and ask for light, love and happiness to pour into your movements.

See? It's pretty easy. You're just being internally intentional before, during, and after you move externally. Also, a quick reminder: you don't need to spend hours working out to achieve results physically, spiritually, or emotionally. 20 to 30 minutes is really all you need. If you follow the framework and pattern, you can move your body daily without burning out.

Movement is an art. You can't rush art. Aligned with the highest frequency, I love using all my senses when I move. Feel the air through your hair, the contractions, expansions, high, lows, shapes, lines, angles, lifting, articulations, momentum, and reaching. Feel your heart beating and your breath releasing. All of this in combination with divine design draws you closer God. This brings euphoria, orgasmic ecstasy, and bliss that truly moves your soul. Can you feel it just by reading this? Doesn't it just make you want to get up and move?

Ponder how you have seen the spiritual and physical linked in your faith journey. Are there ways you need to change how you're taking care of your body in order to take care of your spirit? Are you being authentic and intentional about the way you move your body, or are you doing it just to do it?

Move how you need to. Move so you can feel good. Move to elevate your vibration. Move to create new space and energy for you to live in. Move to wake up, be alive, and to become unstuck. Move to get out of the ego. Move to LIVE WILD! Move to feel empowered & enlightened. Move to celebrate who you truly are. Move to welcome yourself home to your own skin. Move to create health. It's hard to feel bad about a body, mind, and soul that you are taking care of. Move because you love your body and you love God, and because the Divine gave you this sacred body to make moves.

Yes, make moves. Not in the "right" way, but in the Divine way. Let's gather the courage to let it all go and not be so concerned about our righteousness that we forget about our wholeness. This way of moving helped me thrive during a time in my life when I felt like I was just surviving. Learning to move in this way is what saved my life, and I believe it will save the lives of my children, their children, and the world. Shift the paradigm of how we move our bodies. See your legacy in motion.

What are you waiting for? Let's begin to recalibrate our bodies. Move and be moved!

What insights, inspiration, and ideas came to you while you read this chapter? Make some notes below:

_____

_____

_____

_____

_____

_____

_____

_____

_____

_____

_____

_____

_____

_____

_____

_____

_____

_____

_____

_____

_____

Chapter 8

THE GURU IS WITHIN

By: Mariah Slingerland

Like so many people, my path to learning how to commune with the Divine began with a wake-up call. My wake-up call felt tragic, devastating, and rocked me to my core. It had me on my knees more times than I can count, but it was necessary. Sometimes we need something to jolt us awake and give us a shove down the path of self-discovery.

Spirituality is getting in touch with your spirit. My path to spirituality is individual—it is unique to me. Once we make the connection from the Divine to our soul, our mission and gifts become realized. Here's how it happened in my life.

One night, I had a dream that my son and I were at a store and I lost him. He had completely disappeared. I ran through the store, frantically calling his name, desperate to find him and, in the dream, I remember having to go home without him. He was always the child that was glued to my leg whenever we went anywhere. Now I realize that, somehow, we knew what our destiny was.

A few days later, he left my house to go live with his father full time and when they drove away, I knew he wouldn't be back to spend the night with us for a long, long time. He needed to be with his dad and this is the way the universe wanted it. I knew it to my core. I could fight, but I loved him too much, and no matter what I tried, I knew—despite what everyone else thought—what was happening. This became my wake-up call.

Every night before bed, I would sit on my couch, close my eyes, breathe, and imagine myself in the clouds. My son would show up, tuck himself under my arm, and tell me about his day. This continued for days, weeks, and years.

Weeks went by before I got to see him in person for the first time since he had left. It was Mother's Day, and he had made me a card. Inside, he had written the words, "Every night I get your Hugs." From that moment, I felt like everything was going to be fine. But every time I had to take him back to his father's house, the pain would start all over again. This was a wound that was going to take every ounce of my strength to heal.

On the physical level, my body was breaking from all the grief, sadness, and shame that I was carrying. I was suffering from extreme headaches, numbness in my hands, swelling in my legs and, at times, I couldn't even walk up the stairs. Western medicine had no answers for me. While in the doctor's office, my doctor offered one more test I could try and something came out of my mouth that shocked me.

"Can't you see I'm dying of a broken heart?" I blurted out.

When I heard it, I knew it was the truth. I was going to have to be my own medicine. My heart was broken and Western medicine didn't have what I needed to heal. That night, I cried one of those deep, ugly-but-the-most-beautiful, necessary cries. I was on my knees begging for the pain to go away, begging for help, begging for peace. Thankfully, help was on the way.

A friend of mine suggested I go see a woman who practiced a form of energy healing known as reiki. I had never heard of it, but I was desperate, broken, and willing. From the moment the woman put her hands on me, my life took a radical turn. It was as if, for the first time, the skies had opened and there was a voice communicating with me. It wasn't usually in our physical words, although sometimes it would be, but it was a communication on an entirely new level–on the level of my soul. What I was begging and praying for was not only coming to save me, it was going to show me how I would someday be able to help others. I instantly understood how the body holds emotions and feelings like grief, guilt, shame, anger, anxiety, depression, and trauma, and I knew that I was being woken up to help others heal. My path was clear, but first I had to heal myself.

We receive knowledge from gurus, teachers, and books. When we take that knowledge and have our own experience with it, this now becomes our wisdom. For the next nine years, I learned. Implementing what I was learning and testing it to see if it worked for me was how I gained wisdom. In the next nine years, I earned twelve energy healing certificates and became a yoga instructor, ordained minister, meditation teacher, and certified spiritual counselor. Over eight trips to India, a trek in the Himalayas, countless tears and healings, I knew that all of it was necessary—all of it leading me and guiding me to never give up. Every experience led me back home to my truth—my true nature–and my soul was awakened. Words fall short when I try to explain the faith that I developed and the truth that I learned. I began to understand the secrets of the universe and how simple it all is. One of my favorite quotes by Nikola Tesla: "If you want to find the secrets of the universe, think in terms of energy, frequency, and vibration." This was my truth.

How is energy developed in a physical space like a temple or church or in the human body? I focused all my energy into learning about it. If I wanted to create with the Divine, I first had to develop the capacity to receive the Divine. The power of sound became my main source of healing; more specifically, chanting. Chanting mantra became the fastest and easiest way for me to connect to the divine through my soul. Chanting is soul talk and it was communicating with my soul, creating an energy or vibration within me, waking me up. This is what I came to understand as my truth. I developed a daily practice of chanting particular mantras to call or connect to the energy or characteristic of that mantra in order to wake up or develop it within me. It was all so simple. It took dedication, devotion, and love on my part, but that is really all that was needed.

The word mantra broken down is "man", which means "mind," and "tra" which means "through". When we say a mantra with all of the love in our heart, we pierce through the thinking mind (ego) and become that mantra. I started to notice that the connection I would feel inside my heart was the most comforting feeling I had ever known. My life still had its normal ups and downs but what I began to realize was that in having daily devotion and dedication to myself, I was developing these tools as energy that would help me with anything that came my way. When meditators first begin a practice, it's only during meditation that they feel peace and love. Over time, my whole day felt peaceful—as if I were in meditation.

Another thing that became noticeably different was how I would react to situations—rather, how I would *not* react. My world started to change. My experiences were changing so everything around me changed too. The more my inside world changed, the more my outside world changed. The more aware I became, the more awareness I would have. It always started with me doing the work first, putting myself first on my list of things to do for the day. If I skipped my practice, my day would be noticeably different. Each night, as I rested my head on my pillow with my hands clasped together, I revisited my blessings of the day. This is what came naturally for me. At this point, I had read, listened, and tried to emulate the countless ways others connected to the divine, but my way had to come naturally through me. It was a constant surrender, allowing, and never giving up the lifestyle that I had developed.

One of my favorite examples of co-creating with the Divine happened when I was about to take a trip to India with some friends. I knew that going to the Golden temple and visiting my guru, Sri Sakthi Amma, was something that was necessary for my growth. It would help me develop the strength and courage to do what I was on earth to do and to gain the wisdom necessary to serve others. The temple gave visitors the opportunity to purchase a cow, a *ghomata*, and donate it to a family. This holy cow could support a family in a multitude of ways: ghee could be used for sacred ceremonies like pujas, while patties could be used to fertilize the land or burned to produce vibuthi, which is sacred ash that helps heal the body. The cow is the only female animal that can produce enough milk to feed all of humanity. Think about the significance of that for a moment.

I wanted the friends that were coming with me to experience the beautiful ceremony done with the *ghomata*, so I decided to raise the funds necessary to buy one. I needed about 775 USD to purchase a *ghomata*. With all the love in my heart, I prayed every day at my outside altar and prayer garden. With my hands together, I prayed, "Please, please, please, God, I really want to buy a cow." Every morning I would get up early, get dressed, go outside, put my hands together, and basically beg. After a few days, I noticed the passion fruit on the vine in my backyard was falling as I prayed. "Please, God, please help me earn enough money to buy a cow," I said as I heard the *plop, plop, plop* of the fruit falling around me. I made a mental note to pick it up after I was done praying.

The next day, more harvest fell, except this time, the sound of the passion fruit hitting the ground sounded like rapid gunfire. My heart was praying and my mind was asking, "Why so many passion fruit?" Then, in this sweet, quiet whisper, I heard an answer to my prayers: "Make jelly."

I immediately found a recipe to make passion fruit jelly and got to work in my kitchen. I handed jars out to all my neighbors. The next day at the altar I continued to pray, "Please, please, please help me buy a cow," and in the background I continued to hear *plop, plop, plop.* I looked up, and out loud I asked, "Hey! Why so many passion fruit?" I was picking up a five-gallon bucket worth of fruit daily. This time, the voice was yelling at me through a megaphone: "Sell the jelly." Ah, okay. I made 80 jars of jelly, put the jelly in an ice chest on my front porch to sell, and in three days I had made enough money to buy a holy cow! When we want something bad enough and that want comes from a place of pure love, the Divine will say yes.

The lessons that I've learned in the last nine years are priceless to me and essential for my growth and deeper understanding of the secrets of the universe—which aren't all that secret if you learn how to connect to them. I tried many ways to connect and once I found what worked for me, everything started to click. From there, I applied everything I had learned into my way of life. I would learn lessons, then take those understandings back to my altar to pray and to ponder until the truth became clear. Here are some of my favorite lessons I have learned over the years:

1. It matters what you say. Your body believes everything you say internally and externally.

2. For every disease man creates, Mother Nature—God—has created a plant that will cure it. Do some research and learn for yourself.

3. When you pray with all of your heart, if what you are praying for materializes, it is the blessing of the Divine. If it doesn't, it was the universe giving you a gift. This is acceptance.

4. When you pray with a problem in mind, the Divine always answers in the form of solutions.

5. The Gospel of Thomas teaches us, "If you bring forth what is within you, what you bring forth will save you. If you do not bring forth what is within you, what you do not bring forth will destroy you." Once I brought forth what was in me to share with the world, my mind found peace and my internal suffering stopped.

6. Dredging up the past is like poking a hornets' nest. You'll get stung every time. The past is the past; it's like a broken pot, just leave it.

7. A temple is a place that receives divine energy. On the physical body, the place that you rub if you have a headache is also known as the temple. The body is a temple and can receive divine energy, but first we must recognize and treat it like a temple.

8. Be like a pelican. Learn to embrace Mother Nature and all that she offers in the form of energy. The pelican saves its own energy by using the energy of the ocean's waves to glide through life and the wind to soar.

9. Truth evolves in us. Just because something is not true for you yet does not make it any less true. Truth is the only thing that lasts forever.

10. Meditation is the mediation between the mind and the soul. We have two lights within us: one is the mind and one is the soul. We can only have one plugged in at a time. Which one is plugged in within you? Meditation means to ponder and to pray means to request.

11. If you can help ease someone else's suffering–especially when you have suffered from that very thing yourself–you should.

12. Karma has everything to do with it. What you put out into the world will come back. Karma from this life is the only thing our soul takes with it into our next life.

13. A *vasana* is a thought that has been put into motion. It comes before karma. The conscious mind has a thought and the subconscious mind says, "Wish granted," and puts that thought into action. This is how our thoughts become our reality.

14. Triggers are our internal intelligence warning us that something isn't right.

15. Forgiveness is the beginning of the healing work. It starts with forgiving the self. How could you not forgive yourself? You didn't know any better. Once you know better and do the same thing, that's on you.

16. Life lessons are like karmas–once you understand a certain lesson, that karma is complete. When a lesson is coming, stand in the middle of the tornado and use your wisdom to not get sucked into it. If you get sucked in, that karmic tornado will come again and again. Learn the lesson and break free from the tornado.

17. The Creator is in the created and that energy is everything.

18. We are all designed to reach the Divine if we so choose. It's up to each individual to choose to cultivate that capacity. No judgment either way.

19. Intention is more powerful than people realize. Be more intentional with your thoughts, words, and deeds.

20. To get from "seek" to "see" you have to erase the "k." K stands for karma. Once you balance your karma, you go from being the seeker to the seer. Good deeds balance karma and you can start today.

21. Everything that we experience physically in the form of injuries, diseases, and cancers happened mentally or emotionally a long time ago. The physical body can and will hold on to unprocessed traumas until you are ready to deal with them. I've seen this mind-body connection with every person I've been blessed to do energy healings with.

22. Personally, this is the most important life lesson: what you are seeking is already within you. The guru is within. After eight trips to India, I realized that on every trip I was looking for someone–my guru–to tell me what my gifts were, what it is that I am meant to share with the world, and what within me is begging to be expressed. Years later, I was in a session telling the person in front of me, who was on that same quest of wanting to know her gifts, exactly what they were. It was my "ah-ha" moment. What I was seeking was me all along.

Knowing the Divine is within me and within all of us is the truth. If you want to see life differently then you simply need to change the way you see things. What people are reflecting to you is where your energy is vibrating at, which is to say, what you experience in your daily life is actually in your hands. Be your own scientist and develop the perfect recipe for your soul's growth and your entire life will change.

Mine certainly did.

What insights, inspiration, and ideas came to you while you read this chapter? Make some notes below:

_____

_____

_____

_____

_____

_____

_____

_____

_____

_____

_____

_____

_____

_____

_____

_____

_____

_____

_____

Chapter 9

YOU LEAD, I'LL FOLLOW

By: Liz Stone

When Keira Poulsen of Freedom House Publishing and I met recently, I was fascinated to find out that we were both creating a healing center. Upon sharing further, we realized that, though they had different missions, they were both the product of a vision based on our own experience and were being created with the Divine. I knew then that our connection would be important. When she reached out to me about collaborating for this book, I felt immediately that I needed to be a part of this work.

Creating with the Divine is how I have been able to bring some of the most important pieces of my mission forward—pieces that are so big that it is only through this collaboration with God that it becomes possible. I've noticed a pattern co-creating in this way. There is a moment, after the initial inspiration, where you know it is far beyond yourself and your ability. There is a moment of choice where you can either put it down and walk away or surrender to the possibility, without any idea of how it is to be done. Stepping into collaboration begins with being willing.

I am getting more comfortable with this rhythm—this knowing in the unknowing. But it wasn't always so. It is a pattern I learned in one of the darkest moments of my life. One I had to learn to navigate while being held captive, for the second time in my life. This time, however, I was being held captive to fear.

In 2005, while attending an event for youth as an adult leader, I had what could only be termed as a breakdown. It began with a panic attack. I attempted to retreat to the room where I was staying but it was followed by another panic attack, and then another, coming in waves until I was lying in the fetal position on the grass outside the barracks where I was staying. I was completely shut down, in a state of collapse, unable to move. I had lost the ability to speak, only my mind was screaming. Unable to communicate or even understand my needs or my terror, I felt trapped inside. Surrounded by others who didn't know how to help me, I laid there, frozen, until someone finally contacted my husband to come pick me up.

When Steve finally arrived, he came walking up to where I was lying. I'll never forget looking up at him in that white "Superman" T-shirt he always wore. My "Superman," as I often joked. *Now everything will be okay,* I thought to myself. I was so grateful that he was there and that I would soon be back in the "safety" of my bedroom. Little did I know that those four walls would become my whole world for a time.

I was diagnosed with PTSD and agoraphobia—an extreme or irrational fear of entering open or crowded places, of leaving one's own home, or of being in places from which escape is difficult. Over the next few days, weeks, and months, memories began bubbling to the surface, along with waves of panic. I remembered the murder of one of my best friends and her mother while I was in high school, the weeks I spent in the psych ward after attempting suicide, and being raped by a childhood friend on my high school graduation trip just weeks after my release from my stay at the psychiatric hospital. Then came the flashbacks of being held captive by my then fiancé in the basement apartment we shared when I moved out on my own at seventeen.

I was plagued by memories of events that I had never told anyone. They were memories that I had locked inside of myself, shrouded by shame. They all came rushing to the surface, never to hide again. I had lost the ability to pretend. I had run from it all. I ran until there was nowhere left to run. Now, surrounded by just the four walls of my bedroom, I was captive once again, this time to all the unresolved fear, shame, and pain of my past.

I was afraid to be alone. Even closing the shower door was too much of a separation from my husband. He and my two young daughters had become my entire world. Anyone else in my space was too overstimulating and I would panic, often having to retreat from the interaction.

Upon prodding, I began to see a counselor. I was hesitant because I thought they would hospitalize me again. I didn't want to leave my family. Steve and I had a deal—he wouldn't allow me to be admitted and I agreed to stay. To stay in this life. To keep breathing. Keep trying. My end of the bargain began to be too heavy at times, however, and I often wondered how I would continue to live beyond each day. It became too difficult so I began to focus by the hour, even minutes. I became overwhelmed by the fact that there were 24 hours in a day—many of which I was awake, struggling to sleep, as fear gripped my world. Existing in this way was excruciating and I knew I couldn't hold on forever.

I will never forget the day I sat in the counselor's office when she told me that she didn't know how to help me. I just sat there, staring at her with what I'm sure was a blank, confused, and destitute face. I had just got done telling her, after her prodding to open yet more doors to reveal some deep, dark secret that I didn't have any more doors. I had shared all that I knew of my past that haunted me.

It was enough, believe me. Finally, she took a sharp breath in and, after exhaling, looked me in the eye.

"I just don't know what else to do for you," she said.

I believed her.

It wasn't her fault, I told myself. I am broken and no one can help me. I am too far gone, it was too much, and now I have to find a way to carry this. The only problem? I was a young wife and mother. Being raised by a mother who struggled with mental illness when I was a child was hard. I didn't want my kids to grow up without me. So, what now? *How can I do this life?* I asked myself.

My days were full of coping. I honestly felt that "this too would pass." I just needed to rest, to stay home and "heal," as if I had some sort of a cold. One day, I was sitting on the couch next to Steve when a wave of panic washed over me. "Help me!" I called out involuntarily. It didn't take long to realize that, as much as Steve wanted to help me, he couldn't reach the terror inside of me. I had to continue to look outside my home. Maybe someone else could help.

I began to see a Cranial Sacral therapist who had helped me with some back pain previously. I had had enough of psychiatrists and counselors from my days as a youth in the psych ward. I had found that road to be circular and my time with the therapist after my breakdown had solidified that in my mind. I needed a different type of therapy. This guy had helped with my back and taught me a lot about natural healing. *Maybe he could help me. If not, surely his brother, who practiced as a homeopath, could,* I thought.

After a few sessions, I felt my hopes dwindling as the panic continued. Steven would drive to the appointment and I would shake and cry on the table while the therapist did the bodywork, and then I would get back in the car to retreat home where I could fully exhale. It was terrible, but it was all I had.

Then one day, a neighbor stopped by and asked, "Can I sit with you?"

Have I become that person? I asked myself as my ego bucked, feeling embarrassed, yet needing and longing for the company at the same time. Still, this was a woman I had come to call a friend, and I was grateful to have her help me break up my day while my two young girls were playing in the backyard.

I was incapable of small talk at this time so we spoke only in spurts as she held my hand. As the waves of panic came, I grabbed at the cordless telephone by my side. I always carried it around since Steve had gone back to work. In my panic, I had instinctively picked up the phone to get help, as if I had just spotted a fire and was calling for a firetruck. I didn't know what I would say. I only knew that I needed help and that I didn't feel I would survive the coming wave.

"Who are you calling?" she quietly asked.

"I don't know." I paused. "Maybe the guy who's been helping me with my back," I answered. Her reply rung in my mind and I have thought of it several times since.

"Does he have the answers?" she asked, looking at me thoughtfully, perhaps even lovingly.

It landed like a ton of bricks. *Oh no! No one can help me,* I thought, my heart sinking with the realization. I felt utterly alone in that moment, even as my friend held my hand in support. I knew that, just like Steve or anyone else in my life, she couldn't really help. She couldn't really reach me. No one could. My desire to end my life increased and I began to plot out how I could die without hurting my family. If only I could find a loophole in the universe that would allow me to leave and not cause them pain.

After she left, my two girls came bounding inside for a snack. I remember looking at them from across the room, loving them as if I were already gone. I felt sadness that I could barely contain and, at the same time, joy at their presence and their light in the room. Could I really live for them? Could I breathe for them?

As they ran back outside, their temporary needs now satisfied, I walked back toward my bedroom. I felt resolve coming over me and it spilled out my eyes, stinging as it did. I would make one final plea. For their sake, I would try. I knew I couldn't live like I had been, in a space of coping. I needed something to hold onto. Something that would not move.

Desperate for answers, I hit my knees. Literally. Not in a graceful and pious position but in a sobbing, pleading mess on the floor. I pleaded for what felt like hours. I begged to have the terror removed from my mind and body.

First came the bargaining. "If you help me get out of this living hell, if you'll heal me, I'll do ANYTHING you want me to do." I meant it.

Then came a promise. "If you will lead me in how to move forward, how to keep moving, keep breathing, keep loving, keep living… I will follow."

I felt prompted to begin writing in a journal. I only wrote when I was feeling positive or receiving inspiration to move forward. As I look back now, I know that I could have benefited greatly from writing the fears and processing my feelings as well but, at the time, I felt too fragile. When I was feeling inspired, I wrote, and when I was feeling overwhelmed, I would read the words that I had written. It was my way of surviving each day and, as I realize now, receiving next steps.

Over time, I began to set goals to venture back out into the world. Not all at once, of course, but bit by bit. I first started with standing on my back deck. I can't describe how open and vulnerable it felt to stand there, hearing the planes overhead or the neighbor's lawn mower, and just *be* without giving in to the desire to run back inside.

My next step was going out to the mailbox. This was an even bigger feat. Not because of the distance from my door, although that was a thing, but because it came with the added "danger" of seeing a well-intentioned neighbor that might see me and want to talk. I was still struggling to not feel overwhelmed by conversations with others and it took some time before I would seek out their company. Then— short trips to the store, with Steve of course. Next came driving around the block myself as Steve encouraged me and reassured me that he could take over at any time. Little by little, I was able to push back the walls of my world.

Going back out into the world was only a priority for me because of my children. I wanted them to have a healthy life and I didn't want them to pick up on my fear. My goal, in fact, was to "get over it" before they grew up enough to realize something was wrong with mommy.

I exposed myself over and over, in the safety of Steve's presence, to things I couldn't do before. I was always pushing myself to be able to stay longer than the last time. It was like athletic training. Bit by bit, my exposure and resilience began to win. As I learned to cope in this way, I began to feel stronger and realize that I could survive my panic. I could survive a racing heart. I could survive.

As a family, we felt inspired to sell our home. We began to talk about this dream of having animals and a piece of land where life was simpler. I laugh at the simpler part of that idea now. Having animals is not easy and sometimes does not feel simpler. We would go to local farm stores with our young girls and talk about what it would be like to build our own little homestead. We began to speak power into it and I started a vision board. First with a few pictures here and there and then, over time, I compiled a whole collage of what the house would look like and how our property would be laid out. Focusing on what I wanted in this way gave me more hope and I began to feel lighter and more capable. God was beginning to teach me how He works in my life. We were collaborating on the next step.

We did get that homestead shortly after and, amazingly, it looked just like the picture I had cut out, complete with a wraparound porch and the corral off to the side of the home. Over the next 6 years, we built that homestead as a family. We raised animals and grew a garden, preserved food, and cooked from scratch. I took long walks with my dog Sammy at my side and began writing my story for the first time in that fertile environment. I began to work on forgiveness. I sat on the porch and watched the birds fly over the open pasture behind our home and watched the cycles and rhythms of nature. I also began to volunteer and found great satisfaction in serving others. It was a time of healing for me as I spent most of my days with my hands and feet in the dirt, working around our home. I didn't realize just how healing it was and how far I had come until I left that space. Still, it was not meant for us to stay forever. Soon we began to feel it was time for a change.

Once again, we felt prompted to sell our home and move on, though we didn't know what was next. At first, we wanted to move down south where it was warmer. Soon Steve began interviewing for jobs in the area. We even met with a realtor there and looked at many properties in different areas. But we couldn't get clear on what area to pursue with our home search so, once again, we began to pray earnestly about where we should go. "Where would YOU have us go Lord?" we asked. The answer came as a surprise. It was so foreign to anything I would have dared for myself that I immediately trusted it. I was beginning to recognize how He spoke to me and could feel when it was larger than myself.

The answer? We should serve a humanitarian mission before we found our next home. I was to reach out to the anti-trafficking organization that I had been volunteering with at the time to see if we could serve with them in any capacity.

They told us that they were looking for someone to go serve at an orphanage in Haiti. Once we made the decision to go, selling our home and 80 percent of our belongings came very quickly. We rented a storage unit for the rest of our stuff and planned for our departure.

To write this now, I am in awe of the relationship I had forged in those dark days and how it had strengthened my ability to follow future promptings. Getting on a plane to fly to Haiti was so far out of my comfort zone that, once again, I trusted—knowing that to be that far beyond myself meant that I could surrender to the fact that I couldn't control what happened. It was His. I had begun to find comfort in that discomfort—knowing that I was being carried by the Divine. What safer place is there?

While in Haiti, we had many experiences that confirmed this belief, including a sleepless night during Hurricane Mathew when it rolled through the Caribbean, devastating the island to the south of where we were living. After two months however, we knew that it was time to return home.

Our time organizing and building files for the children at the orphanage had given great insight into our next step. As grateful as we were for the rescues that the anti-human trafficking organization was doing, we knew that our time could best be spent in the prevention and aftercare side of human trafficking. My mind would often flash to seventeen-year-old me, leaving home so unprepared, and the painful experiences that followed.

What if we could prepare the kids aging out of the orphanage? I thought. What if we could provide them with a mentor to walk with them as they learn to navigate life in the community? What if we could provide trauma therapy so that they could build a life different from anything they had been taught or exposed to? The mission for

Empowering the One was taking shape. And something else was beginning to take shape at the same time. We were meant to adopt. Upon arriving home, we began the long adoption process.

In 2018, we launched our program with 20 youth aging out of the orphanage in Haiti, providing a mentor, education, and helping them to transition safely to the community with trauma therapy and an opportunity to serve others.

Nothing about our work in Haiti is easy. We have countless ups and downs. We face challenges of severe poverty, gang violence, political instability, transportation strikes, etc. In the past year, their president was assassinated and the country has been in a sort of limbo due to country lockdowns. There are starts and stops as each new challenge arises. Still, the Haitian people are some of the most resilient people I have ever known and they teach me daily.

Through my work there, and now stateside with a Haitian team of mentors and an in-country director, I have seen many cycles of this instability and am more comfortable in the unknown. I've often wondered why God sent me to Haiti. Lots of people go to Haiti. It is the NGO capital of the world, after all. But why me? What do I have to learn through my connection to this amazing island in the Caribbean? I'm still learning, but if I had to guess, I'd say resilience in the face of not knowing. Moving forward in the face of impossible odds, knowing you are not in charge. Learning that every day is one of creating an initial plan, correcting as you go, and standing in acceptance and even gratitude at the end result, which so often is nothing like what we had planned. "This or something better," as the saying goes. I learned this in Haiti. Leaning in, trusting, surrendering, and showing up consistently with a willing heart—ready to learn.

With each of these experiences, I had to continue to lean into the inspiration of next steps, realizing it was far greater than anything I had ever done or knew how to do. I've been learning that the knowing how part is almost irrelevant until I have made a decision to move.

Once I surrender and step into trusting in inspiration's voice, I receive the "how." It is never revealed all at once. The Lord knows me too well. I'm a known runner! In order to avoid scaring me off, He reveals the next step bit by bit as I walk warily forward, asking to be led and only receiving what is relevant at the time.

In early 2020, as COVID-19 began to change our way of life, we finalized our adoption and brought our son home just 4 months shy of his 18th birthday. We were so excited to finally all be together. By summer of that same year, however, I hit the edge of my capacity in healing again. I couldn't believe it, as far as I had come, thoughts of ending my life began to creep in again. Then, right on its tail, so much guilt.

Who am I to feel this way? I thought. I have such a beautiful life. An amazing supportive family. A purposeful life doing work that matters. I have the opportunity to speak and share my story of moving back into the world after trauma and creating purpose. But it didn't matter.

"Where are you God?" I asked. "I can't do this work or this life surrounded by this darkness." I began to feel the weight on my chest and my heart began to ache. Was I waking up to this feeling or was it new? No, I recognized this ache. My mind began to slide back into the old story. I must be too broken. Maybe I never did heal but rather just found another way to survive. *I am a survivor, but this way of surviving isn't survivable,* I thought.

Desperate for answers, I hit my knees, but this time the conversation was different. It was much franker. It was one of negotiation, but also one of resolve with the beginnings of unattachment. It was the unattachment that got my attention.

"I can't live like this," I told Him. "I won't survive it anymore. I can't. I want to die. I know that Steve will be okay, but my kids, Lord—what about my kids? How can I continue to carry this after all these years?" I asked. "Will you help me? I don't know what to do. I only know I can't do this!"

To be honest, I only reached out for help because of my daughter. I had recently learned that she too was struggling and, in watching her, my own pain and guilt rose to the surface. I had begun to lose hope for myself but maybe I could find help for her. I began searching and, after many calls, I found someone who agreed to meet with her in person. This was a big deal because the pandemic had altered so many things and seeing a therapist in person was difficult. After a long phone conversation in which I basically interviewed him, I hung up the phone. My experience with counselors in the past had made me leery of signing my daughter up for the same hope/crash cycle.

Sitting alone in my office, I kept hearing my last words to him. "Oh, and I may need to talk to you too." I hadn't meant to say that. I wasn't looking for me. I felt resigned to my experience and was starting to go numb. I had become anti-therapist and definitely anti-male therapist. But, somehow, I had felt that hope begin to rise in me in spite of my fear. The quiet thought floated into my mind and heart. *What if he could help me too?* After all, I had specifically tracked him down because he did EMDR (Eye, Movement, Desensitization, and Reprocessing). I had studied about it and learned that it had great results with PTSD and processing traumatic memory. Maybe, just maybe, I could try. Still, no commitments to live. Just a willingness to show up and try.

Over the next year and a half, I worked weekly with Jeff. I joke now that I knew he was the therapist for me when he walked in wearing flip flops. I am known for being a barefoot girl and over the last couple years have worn my flip flops year-round when I wear shoes at all.

Still, it took time for trust to grow and, week by week, I stepped in tentatively. Although I had laid out "the big stuff" early on, I was always hesitant to process them with EMDR. As I did however, I began to feel relief and hope rising once again.

Then, a decision. It felt a bit like "cheating" on my therapist to admit it, but I still had not ruled out ending my life at that time. The day I woke up knowing that I couldn't go any further unless I committed to my healing and "putting it down" (as Jeff called it), I went for a long drive. I ended up at the reservoir near my home and had a very frank conversation with God.

"If I'm going to live this life, then I am going to have to live differently. I cannot walk around breathing and carry this much pain. I'll do this if you'll walk with me." I was finally willing but knew I couldn't do it alone. I needed commitments from God. I needed support. I needed strength.

Week by week, we worked through memories and experiences as they came up in our sessions. Sometimes I would pull back. "I feel like I'm barely holding on," I told Jeff. He was aware of my suicidal ideation at this point. "I can't carry it," I said.

"You say that like you aren't already carrying it. Like it isn't the filter that you walk around with every single day. You're already carrying it," he told me. "What would that look like to put it down?"

His words stung with truth and I thought of the terrain I had crossed over the last 30 years carrying that pain. I thought of my plea to God to take it from me or let me die. I thought of my growing family and the legacy I would leave. Once again, I felt myself settle into a place of surrender. I would continue to do the work.

Over the next several months we processed through the unresolved traumas I had been carrying. Growing up, my parents' divorce, my mother's mental illness and alcoholism, being raped by a childhood friend, losing Maureen and her mother when they were murdered by Maureen's sister's estranged husband, being held captive in that basement apartment with the threat that if I left, he would find me and kill me and my family. How I believed him and remembered what happened to Maureen. How I ran that day when my friend and neighbor, Chris, showed up at my door and how, emotionally at least, I never looked back. How I buried it all deep—so deep—that it was the seed that grew into major dysfunction in my life. A reality that, no matter how far I ran, how many relationships I had, how much I drank, or how hard I worked, I could not escape. This time however, I stayed in there. I didn't run. I cried and shook and allowed my body to unwind, asking for and receiving help from God as I did.

Although I had the support of Steve and my children, a committed and knowledgeable therapist, and daily support from angels, I began to feel heavy. My work in Haiti had also hit turbulent times when we had to report abuse to the child authority division for some of the youth in our program that had aged out of the orphanage. As we did, we began to get so much resistance and were no longer safe to travel to that location.

Feeling drawn to balance the heaviness of life, I began to talk to Steve about running away again. Not as I had in the past but just on vacation or to a deserted island. "Let's just sell it all and buy a bus" has been code our entire marriage for "I'm really hurting and need some stress relief." Luckily, we didn't have to run too far. Some friends of ours own a stone and crystal shop and we had often talked about how fun it would be to start a shop in our hometown. I had grown to love stones and crystals as I learned about how grounding they could be. I also found value in carrying around a stone in my pocket to hold and distract myself with when feeling anxious. Remembering that our friends would be in a neighboring state at a huge show with vendors from all over the world, we decided to go.

I had an appointment with Jeff the day before we left town. I was a bit hesitant to tell him at first, thinking he may feel that I was avoiding life and "running away." The idea of starting a stone and crystal shop seemed so frivolous to anything I was doing in my life at the time and I almost felt guilty. "It's not avoidance if I'm doing the work, right?!" I joked with him.

Smiling, Jeff responded, "I think it's a great idea. But only if you come back with a sunflower dress!"

Walking around and learning about the different vendors and stones, I began to feel that prompting again. "This could be possible!" I kept saying to Steve. Before the weekend was over, we had loaded the back of our Subaru and the decision was made. We were starting a new business. On the way back through town we stopped at a small shop that had a for rent sign and, by the time we left, we had signed a lease to start our new shop. Our kids just smiled and shook their heads when we told them. They had gotten used to seeing me get an inspiration, acting on it, and changing directions and life paths many times. "Of course, you did!" was all one my daughters said, smiling.

As I continued my work in therapy with Jeff, I began to build our new shop. Stepping into creativity was a way for me to balance the heaviness of my own processing and all that was going on with our work in Haiti. I also began to feel another emotion coming to the surface as I worked through and began to let go of the fear, pain, and shame that I had been carrying. This emotion was different. It was bittersweet. Along with the gratitude that I felt for having been led through my healing, I began to grieve.

I began to grieve for the 30 years it's taken me to get to this point. To be honest, the first 15 years I actively avoided anything to do with my trauma, but for the last decade and a half, I have actively been pursuing resources and answers. But I didn't know where to look. I didn't know what was possible. I had wished for a mentor— a guide. Now that I was studying and processing trauma, learning about other healing modalities, I kept having one thought.

"I wish I had done this earlier," I often told Jeff. "What else could have been possible over the last 30 years if I had known that I could have healed years ago?" I'm still working on forgiving myself and my path and learning to accept it.

The promptings began to come. What if I could create what I had needed? What if we could create a center where these and other trauma informed resources were available to help people heal? What if we could create a community where people could connect and no longer feel alone? Then, the painfully obvious reality. I didn't know how to build such a center.

Still, the idea wouldn't go away. It bounced around in my head and so I asked. "Is this your will, Lord? If I move, will you help me?" Again, I continued to be inspired. "Okay, Lord. You lead, I'll follow."

Our healing center is now a reality. I have the most amazing conversations in our shop about what else is possible. I hear stories of heartbreak and trauma and feel the hopelessness and despair of those who share so courageously. I also see the willingness to believe there could be something different and the courage to trust as they step out to try something new.

As I tell people at the center, I don't know the right next step for you or anyone else. I only know that there *is* a next step. There *are* answers. Hope and healing are possible. Healing is not linear, at least it hasn't been for me. However, you will recognize what is right for you as you are open to it. Something will begin to resonate with you. And so, it starts. Hope sparks.

But, as I have painfully learned, hope without resources is devastating. This is not how the Divine works. That hope is followed by a flash of light and inspiration. It is only when we are at the edge of our own capacity that we step into that of the Divine. It is sacred ground. Unknowing is not to be feared but to be embraced. We are not meant to know it all and to see the end from the beginning. That is not our part. When we turn our lives over to God in faith, focusing on what we want rather than what we fear, forgiving ourselves, others, and circumstances, we are free to move forward and fulfill all that he has for us. Trust him. Take two steps into the darkness of the unknown, lean in, listen with a willing heart, and light will appear.

As I do this in my life, the right mentor, path, modality, or even book shows up for me. My hope is that this book will be that for you—a confirmation that you are seen and heard. You are capable. That desire that is swirling in your heart is there for a reason; it is an invitation. Co-creation is a two-sided effort. You are never alone, for you, my dear, are co-creating with the Divine.

What insights, inspiration, and ideas came to you while you read this chapter? Make some notes below:

_____

_____

_____

_____

_____

_____

_____

_____

_____

_____

_____

_____

_____

_____

_____

_____

_____

_____

_____

Chapter 10

GUARDIAN ANGEL

By: Amy Hill

I am a mother of 3 adult children and grandmother to 5 amazing little humans. Lilyanna, Maddox, Palmer, Danika, and Slater are the light of my life and the center of my world. I have, for the most part, had a blessed life and was taught about spirituality and God from a young age.

My mother was only 16 years old when she had me. She married my biological father, who was 6 years older than her. My father, however, was abusive, so the marriage only lasted two years. After my mom left, we moved in with her parents. This is where I built my foundation of so much love. My grandparents were kind and adoring and had a relationship with the Lord. They helped set the tone for my life. I have always felt a strong connection with them in so many ways and, even though they are now deceased, I still have a very strong spiritual connection with them.

My mother remarried when I was three and, in less than a year, I had a baby sister. My stepfather adopted me when I was seven and has been the best and only real father I have ever known.

The only religious background I had was from my grandparents. My sister and I would visit them often on weekends and go to church with them. So, by age nine, I decided that I wanted to be baptized into their church (The Church of Jesus Christ of Latter-Day Saints). My parents were supportive of my decision and agreed to take me to church even though they were not members themselves.

As the years passed, I discovered more and more about my spirituality, but it wasn't until six years ago that I really discovered who I am. My journey began when I agreed to an opportunity to learn about a modality of healing called muscle testing. I had contemplated taking this course for over a year but, because of logistics and the cost of the class, it was going to be difficult to make happen. I live in Colorado and the class was going to be held on Tuesday evenings for 12 weeks in Arizona.

At the time, I worked part-time as a dental assistant, but of course one of my work days was Tuesday, and it was always my long day. How could I possibly be in Arizona every week for 12 weeks and still keep my job? The cost of the class was a huge expense for me at the time, and thinking about spending that kind of money on myself felt foreign and selfish. But besides the money, there were other concerns. Where would I stay? Would I rent a car? All I could see were blocks and expenses, but my heart was being pulled toward it and I just knew I needed to make it happen. I prayed and prayed before I finally pulled the trigger and said yes. It was almost like magic as I watched everything fall into place.

After prayerful consideration, I gave my two weeks' notice at the dental office so that I could fully concentrate on this new path and give it my all. I started searching for flights and actually found roundtrip tickets for only $79! I held my breath and booked flights for the next 4 weeks. Holy crap, I was really doing this! In the meantime, I discovered that I had a relative that lived in Arizona and would be attending the class as well. I called her to see if it would be a possibility to stay with her and attend class with her. She was very gracious and not only offered me a place to stay but also a ride to and from the airport. I have a cousin I am close to that lived in San Diego and she decided to take the class as well. We were able to coordinate our flights to come in at the same time so that my aunt in Arizona would only have one airport run to make.

I just knew that God wanted me to be in this class. When I had no idea how to make it happen, He did! God had a plan for me and He was guiding me every step of the way.

During the course of the class, my personal life was taking a dive. I struggled with finances, I struggled with my spirituality, and I really struggled with my marriage. I kept praying for answers but didn't feel like I was receiving what I was looking for. I then had an experience that would change the course of my life forever.

About six weeks into the academy, I was feeling exceptionally overwhelmed by life and was at the lowest I had ever been. My husband and I were fighting so I didn't even want to be at class that night. During the break, one of the facilitators approached me and said that they wanted me to be the student in the chair in front of the whole class after break. For those of you who don't know about this experience, let me fill you in. In a muscle testing session, you sit in a chair and the facilitator sits next to you. You hold up your arm and try to keep it strong. The facilitator asks you yes or no questions and pushes on your arm. Your spirit knows, so if the answer is true, your arm stays strong. If the answer is no, it is weak and goes down. The arm grows weak in the absence of truth.

So, when the facilitator asked me to be the student in the chair, my first reaction was, "Oh, hell no!" I had too much to risk in showing my vulnerability. I didn't want everybody in class knowing my personal business and what was going on with my husband. She asked me to think about it during break, so I went to a quiet place and asked God what He wanted me to do. I asked Him to help me be strong and to do what was best for me and for the class. When break was over, I very timidly said yes to being in the chair. I was terrified, to say the least, but knew I needed to be there.

The first question the facilitator asked was, "Do you know what you're going to uncover today in this session?" I said yes and he asked me what I thought it was. I said, "It's about my relationship with my husband." Much to my surprise, when he pushed on my arm, it was very weak, which meant that was a no! At that point, I was so relieved that I was willing to talk about anything! The session then proceeded with some feelings of guilt and shame with my spirituality. We discovered that it was centered around me leaving the church that I had attended all my life. He then asked if there was a person that was involved with my guilt over leaving the church, and I knew at that moment that it was my deceased grandmother. He asked me to close my eyes and let them roll back and look down into my heart. As I did, tears started streaming down my cheeks. I felt her presence with every fiber of my being. It felt like she was sitting right next to me, and I thought if I opened my eyes, I would see her right there with me. The facilitator then asked if she were disappointed in me, and I received a very strong answer that she was not. I had held onto this guilt and shame for so many years and it was so powerful for me to let it go. I had uncovered something way bigger than I had anticipated and it was a beautiful and powerful moment for me.

After class, I had a woman approach me and ask if she could have a word with me. She explained that she has a gift of being able to see spirits from the other side. She said that she usually sees them in 2-dimension but this time was very different for her. She said that she saw my grandmother standing over my body like an angel, but she was in 3D. As I was clearing the negative entities attached to me, she saw my grandmother gathering in all of the "junk" and taking it from me. She said that my grandmother must have been an amazing woman because she just sparkled. The woman likened her to the fairy godmother in Cinderella. There were sparks flying as my grandmother gathered in all of my pain, took it from me, and sent down fairy dust to protect me. I told her that I felt my grandmother's spirit so strongly and I knew that what she said was true.

The woman then told me that my grandmother had a message for me, and being the curious person that I am, I needed to know! She said that my grandmother wanted me to write a book. I had never in my life considered doing anything of that nature. I mean, who was I to write a book? But this was the beginning of my journey to finding my relationship with the Divine, connecting with angels, and finding the magic that is within.

I started receiving very strong messages from the Divine and from my grandmother after this experience. I remember one day, I was sitting in my sacred space, and I heard once again that I should write a book. I literally laughed out loud and said to myself. "Are ya sure? I am not a writer. This is just a crazy thought." I pushed it away for a very long time, but the idea kept getting stronger and stronger.

As a child, my grandmother always had a lot more confidence in me than I had in myself so I just kept thinking, "I know you have a lot of confidence in me, Grandma, but what will I write?" But it was getting so loud that I knew I had to make this happen. I finally prayed and asked God to tell me what it was He wanted me to share with the world. I told Him that He'd have to give me the words because I had no clue where to start.

I handed it over to God and, when I did, my fingers just started writing and the words just flowed. Before I knew it, I had written my first children's book. It only took about 2 hours to let God tell me what He wanted me to say. My grandchildren illustrated my book, so it is a very special project for all of us.

I am grateful for the experience of working with my angels and the Divine and birthing my first book. I have received messages that there are many more books to be written as well. This is just the beginning of a beautiful journey of working with the Divine.

What insights, inspiration, and ideas came to you while you read this chapter? Make some notes below:

_____

_____

_____

_____

_____

_____

_____

_____

_____

_____

_____

_____

_____

_____

_____

_____

_____

_____

_____

_____

Chapter 11

OF COWS, CREATION, AND CHRIST

By: Suzan K. Manning

I collaborate, communicate, and create with the divine through my own style of poetry. I was blessed to collaborate and receive from the Divine a book of poems titled, "An Angel Stood Before Me."

As I was open to receive them, the poems would flow through me.

As I sat to write this chapter, God showed up again in my writing and transformed my chapter into poetry.

Enjoy!

OF COWS, CREATION, AND CHRIST

Oldest of seven.
Four girls
and
A boy.
In the middle.
The only
son.

Westside
of
Phoenix

An
agrarian
life
of
black
and white
cows.

Holsteins.

For
me the
clarity of
black and white.
The beauty.
The comfort
without
the

Judgement.
Immediate
Recognition.

Clarity
of
Who they were
for me...
Comfort
And companionship.

Baby calves
that held your fingers
in their mouth
as they were learning to drink.

The warmth of their bodies
in a bed
of
Straw.

Not mangers.
But a
Reminder
of
The Divine
just
the
Same.

Time
felt
rich

then
Moving
like
A meandering
River.

Time to
Connect
with
The Divine.

I
didn't recognize it
then
But
I
Knew it.

That
Knowingness
is
like a
handful of
rich soil….
You curl your fingers
around it
And squeeze.
It holds
Together
and you
can see
the indentations

your fingers
and palm
make.

A
Difference.

Then you let
go.
It is gone.
But you can still feel the soil
on your hand.
A reminder.

Magical seeds
called
Words.
Individual
like
Seashells.

When
words come,
they aren't
always
contained.
But
The residue
is there.
The reminder.

The promptings
To write
To express
To witness
of
The
Divine.

Personal
expression
with
The Divine

The
Seeds
and
Seedlings
that
are planted
in
the rich
earth of
my soil.
My soul

The harvest:
A gift
A comfort
A growth
An expression
A witness:

He Lives

What insights, inspiration, and ideas came to you while you read this chapter? Make some notes below:

_____

_____

_____

_____

_____

_____

_____

_____

_____

_____

_____

_____

_____

_____

_____

_____

_____

_____

_____

_____

_____

_____

Chapter 12

COME TO THE EDGE

By: Valerie Bote, RN, BSN

Come to the edge. The magic is waiting
outside of your comfort zone.
Take a leap of faith.

One morning in October of 2021, I had a vision as I was waking up. I saw myself at the edge of a cliff, with my hair blowing in the wind and my arms lifted, as if I was celebrating. I heard a message in my head, which I quickly copied down in my journal: "All you have to do is trust and leap. You are ready. Ride this wave of change. It is time. Let go of fear."

Let go of fear. What does this mean to me? It means everything.

Fear has always been a part of my life. It began in my childhood, where fear was the main driving force of my decisions. As a young child, I was taught to fear everything—from the things I could not see to the people who were supposed to give me love and care. I feared my parents, my caretakers, my teachers, and all my elders. I even feared God.

It isn't surprising that I grew up unable to make decisions for myself without the expressed permission of those around me. I lived my life and made my decisions, big or small, based on my fears.

A life full of fear is paralyzing. Fear is like a darkness. It is like a thick, gray fog that prevents someone from moving forward on a road. When we are enveloped in this thickness, it is hard to see. When we fail to see, we fail to trust. In my life, this lack of trust manifested in several ways: lack of self-worth, the inability to make decisions for myself, always seeking permission and approval from others, and a lot of doubt in my capabilities, resulting in a life lived based on lack—lack of belief in my world and my life.

Living from this perspective of lack, one cannot see, know, or feel with clarity. Disempowering choices stem from this space and perspective. When you believe that authentic power comes from external things, you operate from doing things solely for the sake of external validation. From that vantage or perspective, it is hard to say how or why we really do the things we do. In my case, it culminated in a deep pain and hunger that I unknowingly had which trickled into the way I lived my life. The pain and hunger could not be satiated with food, for it was a hunger for love and validation.

Fast forwarding to today, I am divorced from my husband of 25 years. As sad and "disappointing" as a divorce may sound, the unpleasant situations leading up to my divorce were the catalyst to my ability to see, know, feel, and understand that this life should not be happening against me but, rather, it should happen *for* me. My divorce was the event that began clearing the dense fog of fear that permeated my entire life. It has been my gateway to forgiveness, trust, love, and wholeness.

My life with my husband was everything I had wanted it to be. I married for love and my wedding day was one of the happiest days of my life. Together, we have three beautiful children, and I would not trade them or this part of my life for anything. I truly felt I was destined to be the wife of this man and the mother of my children. I had given up my career, in full agreement with my husband, to be a full-time mother to my children. It was the way I had imagined how to be a mother. Raising my own children and giving them my full attention as their mother was a dream come true. As fortunate as I was to have been able to do this, the life that I thought would be my only path was actually only a small part of the life I was truly meant to live. I can see this now, but I did not know it then. All I knew was that my marriage was crumbling and my husband and I were growing apart.

Looking back, we were two good people who got lost as we grew, trying to fulfill needs and putting Band-Aids on the spots in our hearts that were hurt. We became blinded by misunderstandings. As situations got worse and the space between us grew, it became difficult to remember the love we had between us. Instead, this love was replaced by walls, resentments, and anger. We both ended up being lost in pain, which culminated in the much-needed dissolving of our marriage.

The road to this ending was not a straight path. It was difficult to navigate with big boulders along the way. The biggest obstacle was fear. Fear was, again, defining my decisions and making me hold on to what seemed like a life raft, though this life raft was not saving me—it was drowning me. My fear manifested itself through anger, resentment, and the inability to forgive and love myself. Through all of this, I started leaning into something greater than myself.

Growing up, I was raised Catholic. I always felt a connection to God, and I prayed to the Blessed Mother as if she were my own. I went to Catholic school from elementary through high school, and I remember in second grade, I would go in the chapel to pray in front of the Blessed Mother's statue before school started. I remember admiring my second-grade teacher who did the same thing, so I emulated her ritual. My teacher was a single woman who prayed for a good husband; I remember going to the Blessed Mother statue and reciting the same prayer of, "Please give me a good husband!"

I sit here and laugh at my second-grade self, and how silly this seems to me now, but guess what? I did get a good husband.

Looking back, I see now how divinely blessed I was to have countless experiences I can go back to and draw from. As I learned to navigate out of fear, I found that I had to change my relationship and understanding of what God is to me. I did this by unsubscribing to the God-fearing way of practicing my faith to one that reminds me that God loves me unconditionally. I started to recognize that the God to whom I pray is a loving God—one who embraces my soul in all of its aspects, and is not vengeful or punishing. All I have to do is ask for help and this God of love will help me, guide me, and forgive me as I forgive myself. As I think it, it is already done.

As this journey to love and trust started to unfold, I also discovered the presence of angels in my life. I don't see them; I just feel them. I receive signs and communication from them through number sequences like 222, 444, 555, 1111, etc. As I became curious about the same number sequences I consistently saw throughout the day, I did some research about these numbers and found out that they are one of the ways angels try to get through to us. I learned how to follow the breadcrumbs and listen to my intuition. I started to listen to the intelligence of my heart rather than my busy-thinking and rational mind. The sacred creation of a life full of peace, love, and freedom began as soon as I decided to be open to receiving love and letting go of fear.

Opening up to this perspective allowed me to see that the events of my life that caused me the most pain were also the biggest catalysts for discovering a way to truly love. In the process, the path to healing opened up. This opening has allowed me to realize that there are no mistakes, just lessons. It does not mean that we just bypass acknowledgement of what we are feeling or that we neglect to honor sadness—it simply means that we have a different perspective, which allows for true growth.

In my case, the pattern of death and rebirth has surfaced in my understanding. It is not physical death, but rather a death of the old ways and a birth to a new way. The hardest events have shaped who I am today. They have prepared me to survive and overcome; to be brave and move through my fears, despite what I believed all my life. It has been the act of letting go of the story of being incapable, not enough, powerless, and, most of all, the story of "I can't." This journey has shown me that, when I work with unconditional trust in the Love that holds my life in its palms, I will be okay. The path will appear as I take the first step.

I have learned to let go of resistance brought about by fear. I had to let go of my tight grip of control and collaborate with God in order to bring goodness and love into my life. Surrendering is not easy, and many days I am still confronted by triggers that cause me to doubt. But having anchored myself in the knowledge that I am not alone, I can bring myself back to love every time fear creeps in. I have cultivated ultimate trust. The story of grace, love, and forgiveness is what I have discovered while on this path. It is a kind of love which carries, cushions, transports, lifts me up, and scoops me out of danger each time. In the midst of pain and hardship, I feel I am always lifted. This path is in no way linear. It's a trek with peaks and valleys. The less load we carry, the easier the journey. Letting go of fear is a big load off my back. Some days, fear and doubt may creep back into my mind, but my heart ultimately knows that love is the only thing that lives there. Fear is merely an illusion. Living in it disconnects us from love and unconditional trust.

My message is one of putting love over fear and allowing this magic to unfold. Before this can happen, however, we need a catalyst for healing. Whether it is through my profession, my talents, the story that I share, or my presence in this world, it is my hope that people who need my help will find it. Furthermore, it is my great wish that the building of these Centers of Hope will help all those who are stuck in fear and provide a refuge for those in despair. May this place help bridge the gap and offer a space where everyone can feel listened to, seen for who they truly are, and loved unconditionally.

As human beings, we go through sadness in stages. When little children are sad, they cry, because they don't understand what they are feeling. They just know they need something to soothe themselves—whether they need soothing in their bellies, their minds, or their hearts. It is the same with adults, but adults can articulate. Sometimes, adults express themselves through rebellion. They express themselves with words that hurt. They express themselves in violence, either to themselves or others.

I have come to realize that we are just souls that came here to learn. Some souls come to learn for a short time and some require a longer time to learn the lessons they have come for. It is not our job to dictate the lessons the soul has come to understand. Our only job is to offer time, space, and a listening ear without judgement.

There are many who are in so much pain they feel they cannot take it any longer. They are surrounded by such a dense fog that they cannot imagine what is beyond it. They naturally want to go back to what they know—to the comfortable and what they've already seen. But if we just hold on and adventure beyond that fog, the beauty of what is on the other side may be discovered. And while I may not dictate what a soul has come here for, or how long, please stay awhile. Keep going. Keep moving forward. You are not alone.

Do we co-create with this life force from the moment we are born or do we co-create after we remember who we truly are? To you who are on this path, to you who are in the midst of pain, to you whom I love, to you who are also questioning if there is more, I want to share this writing from my heart and soul.

STAY AWHILE

In the quiet, I can hear

In the stillness, I can feel the stirring of my soul

So much inside me has to come out

So much I need to remember

What have I forgotten?

How have I forgotten?

What plans did I have before I came in this body?

What privilege to be here on earth as a human being.

All the beauty to behold

All the wonders to be told

All the goodness to unfold

I have forgotten.

Without pain, I can think clearly

It was all feeling I am magic

Not one bit tragic

Without the pain, I can feel

My song yearns to be sung

Oh sweet one

Of beauty and magic and unconditional love

It is simple but pure

This song I have—it's buried deep in my heart,
for pain has covered it

My song yearns to be sung

Oh sweet one

Of kindness and understanding that can only be felt when I'm here

There is a message only I can tell

There is a gentleness only I can give

There is a dance only I can dance

In this gift called life

This is the magic that needs to be remembered

So do not leave with your music still in you

You've wanted this

You've yearned for this

Now remember what you have forgotten

You have a message only your heart can share.

What insights, inspiration, and ideas came to you while you read this chapter? Make some notes below:

_____

_____

_____

_____

_____

_____

_____

_____

_____

_____

_____

_____

_____

_____

_____

_____

_____

_____

_____

_____

Chapter 13

WALKING IN FAITH 🦅

By: Keira Poulsen

Collaborating with the Divine… this topic is one of my favorites and one that I treasure deep in my heart. I don't even really know how to begin to write about it. What one story, one experience, or one moment could I possibly choose out of hundreds or maybe even thousands?

I wouldn't be here without God, Christ, the Divine Mother, or my angels. Since I was 14, I have struggled with suicide ideation. The pain inside of me was so intense that leaving this world seemed to be my only strategy for relief. And that is simply what it was—a strategy.

I had become a professional strategist.

As I had been sexually abused many times in my childhood, looking for the strategy to be safe was *essential*. And strategizing out of pain was what I was best at. Suicide was just one strategy to escape the pain I had deep inside me. But so was leaning on the spiritual realm. Each time my brain told me it was time to leave this world, I would reach out to God in a last-sitch effort to stay. And time and time again, I would feel God's love envelop me. I would feel God ease my pain and lift me through the darkness that suffocated me. God was my lifeline.

But I didn't always hear God. I could feel God, and I knew God was real, but I didn't know that there could be a straight line of communication between me and Him until January of 2015.

It was the middle of the night and I was rocking my fifth baby, who was only a month old. My sweet son could barely breathe. He had just been diagnosed with RSV earlier that day. RSV is respiratory virus that can take a baby's life. The nurses told me that there was nothing they could do, and to bring him back to the ER if he stopped breathing. I was terrified. I felt so helpless, so alone, so afraid for my son's life.

I began to plead. I knew God could show me how to heal my son. I just knew it. All I needed was for God to show me what to do. I needed God to speak to me. I intentionally asked that God show me how to heal my baby and help him breathe with ease. And in that moment, a vision—like a movie playing in my mind—appeared. I saw golden light being poured down on my little one's head and I was shown what to do with this light. I was told how to use the light, including using parts of the brain that I didn't even know the names of before that moment. I don't know how long this experience was, but when it finished, my little 4-week-old baby was breathing with ease. God had shown me what to do and had spoken to me through my heart—through words in my mind and visuals that I could only see with my spiritual eyes.

This was the beginning of a new life for me. No longer was God some distant being who would swoop in during my darkest hours; now He was real, tangible, and accessible. Life would never be the same again. This new realization would be very necessary over the next 7 years, as my life would be broken apart in every way possible and I would need to have this clear line of reception open at all times.

I was soon led on a very detailed journey of selling our house. I had five little kids in a very small home, and I had wanted to move for years. A week after I had the experience with healing Jones, I was led, through dreams in the middle of the night, on what to do to sell our home. This seemed crazy as it was during a time where it was impossible to sell a house. No one's home had sold in our neighborhood in ages. Homes stayed on the market for 8 months at a time only to get a low-ball offer and, if they were lucky, a sale. But I was shown exactly what to do.

One night, I had a vision of how to redo our living room to prep it for listing, and I saw a yellow chair. The next morning as I was driving, I had the feeling to turn down a road that was out of my way. I listened to the feeling and there in front of me, in the middle of a yard sale, was the yellow chair I had been shown the night before. It was $25. I cried in gratitude as I placed this chair in my living room. It became my miracle chair. I cried because I knew God was working with me. This was a new relationship, a new connection with the Divine that I had never experienced before. It was sweet and delicious and powerful. For the next few months, I was led on this journey one step at a time. I was led to my dream home on a half-acre. It was $515K, which was ridiculous for us, as a young couple in our early thirties, to even imagine.

I remember going to God and asking how we could pay for this house and I was shown a vision of Moses and his staff. I was shown how Moses could create water by hitting his staff against a rock. I was shown that anything was possible and so I believed.

The next day, we somehow got approved for the loan! And that is how the whole experience went. Moment after moment, day after day, I witnessed God's miracles. I began to council God on all things, as I knew He would now answer. I asked what day our house would sell, and I saw that would be on June 13th. That felt nearly impossible as we were listing our home on June 8th and homes in our area never sold that quickly. But it was no surprise when our house sold on June 13th.

I was giddy. I was so excited that God had been leading me on such an extraordinary path and that we were getting the house of our dreams! Everything was flowing and moving until ten days before our home was supposed to close and the appraisal came in $20k under our asking price. Everything began to crash down around me. We had to back out of the dream house, but we decided to still sell our house because it was an absolute miracle that someone wanted to buy it. But we didn't have anywhere to go, so we ended up moving in with my parents (all 7 of us).

This all occurred within ten days. And I was certain God was a fraud. I started to doubt that God had even spoken to me. I questioned who had been guiding me every day. I knew I was being guided— that I could not doubt—but it couldn't be God. Or so I thought.

I decided that day that there was no God. Clearly God would not lead someone along, only to rip their dream right from under their feet at the last moment. That was so cruel. Surely God would never do such a thing. And so, I went for 24 hours without a God.

It was the first time in my life where I lived in this world without God, and it was painful. It was lonely, bleak, and hopeless.

I remember waking up early the morning after we had found out we would be losing the home on the half-acre and would have to move in with my parents. This was the day I decided God was a fraud. I could feel the suicidal thoughts getting louder, but this time there was no God to save me. I walked to the desert at the end of our neighborhood. It was filled with wild animals, including snakes and scorpions. I laid on the dirt and wished that a rattlesnake would show up. The hopelessness was so real, so intense, and for the first time I had no Divine being above to save me from it.

But nothing happened. No scorpions crawled out of their hidden places and no rattlesnakes slithered by. It was silent and lonely.

I remember that sad walk home. I felt a void in my life without God. I had just experienced 6 months of spiritually walking with God. I had received visions, heard God's voice in my heart, and now I didn't even believe He was real. It was like a part of my heart had been ripped out. I stubbornly chose to push the reality of God out of my life because of the deep pain I felt. How could God have tricked me like this? I felt deceived and hurt.

Yet, 24 hours without a God was so hopeless and so lonely that I chose to believe in God again. I didn't want to live in a world without a God. I chose to believe that all that had happened was for my good. It was simply that… a choice. I believed that, one day, I would see why God had led me to sell my house and why the dream of living on land had crumbled at the last minute.

I would see all of those reasons later, but it would take 5 years (and a lot of breaking and healing) to get me to that point.

For the next 14 months, I felt like I just survived. We couldn't find the right home for months, and when we did, it was a new build. They told us it would take four months to build, but it ended up taking 10 months. So, for 14 months I lived in my parent's home, with all five kids and my husband. It was not ideal. It brought up plenty of old emotions that I hadn't processed when I left their home at age 19. But now I was moving through these feelings while raising five kids! It felt so noisy and chaotic and I didn't really talk to God that much. So, as a result, those 14 months were pretty quiet in regard to receiving visions and communing with God.

I find this to be a powerful lesson in collaborating and communing with the Divine. **Working with God only works if we create the space and time for it.** *If we don't, then it doesn't exist.*

I think that many people believe that God will only speak to them if they are "worthy" or special. But these 14 months negated those beliefs. I wasn't doing anything different than before. I wasn't "unworthy." I wasn't making different choices. I was the same Keira as before.

Before we moved, God was speaking to me every day through thoughts, visions, and inspiration. Then it went silent. 14 months of silence from the Divine, *simply because I wasn't creating the space to ask.* **I didn't ask, so God didn't talk.**

What if that is all that stands between humans and the Divine? Not worthiness like we are so often taught, but instead the simplicity of asking. God created us to have agency, and if we truly have agency and if God abides by that same law, then God respects our agency. If we ask, God will answer. I find that if we ask and take actions based off faith, then God really pours down the answers. When we ask and then sit down and wait without moving, it's like trying to make cookies with no ingredients. It's impossible. Our willingness to take action from faith is the ingredient for God. We must be willing to walk so that He can open the paths in front of us.

The next 3 years made that very clear for me.

There are far too many experiences for me to share, so I have chosen to share my most sacred experiences. I struggled at first to share these. I asked God if it was okay for me to share them and the answer I received was, "I didn't give you these experiences to hold all to yourself. Share, and give them to others." And so, with that, I am grateful to share what happened for me when I began to ask again.

It was my birthday dinner, October 22, 2016 and I was sitting at a booth in a dimly lit Cheesecake Factory with my husband, Dan. I was eating my favorite meal and everything was wonderful—but only on the outside. I had been struggling with depression for the past few months. Even though we had moved into our beautiful new home, designed exactly how I wanted it, I was unhappy. Even though we were finally out of my parent's house and life looked amazing, I was dead inside. I couldn't figure out what was wrong with me. I had everything I had ever dreamed of. And I was more unhappy than I had ever been. There was a lull in our conversation and then Dan asked me, "What are your dreams for this year?" This question proved to be the most Divinely guided question that has ever been asked to me. Immediately, I broke down sobbing. Big, ugly tears in the middle of the restaurant.

I told Dan that I didn't have any more dreams left. *I had forgotten how to dream.* In that moment, Dan spoke words that would forever change my life. He said, "Keira, you have three days to come up with three dreams."

And so, it began. The sincere prayer that I prayed every single day for the next five months. I prayed morning and night, pleading with God that He would show me how to dream again. I prayed that God would show me my purpose here on earth.

And for 5 months, I received nothing. No visions, no thoughts, no words... nothing.

Until February 17th, 2017.

God's answer came in a way I could've never imagined. It came in through massive levels of pain that I never even knew existed. I found out that someone I knew and loved had been sexually abused. In the finding out, it ripped open all of my own childhood trauma of being sexually abused. It was pain that I had tucked away, pushed down, and ignored for most of my life. It was as if a tidal wave that had been gaining speed for 20 years had finally hit me.

The level of pain was so intense that I knew I wouldn't survive. I knew that this time, I couldn't live. As the suicidal thoughts became heavy and extremely tangible, I felt God. He was very distant and very far because it felt like the suicidal entities had taken up most of the space within and around me.

I felt God say that I was needed here on earth. I was being asked to stay. And in that moment, something deep inside of me agreed to stay. And not only to stay, but to *really live*. I agreed that if I was to stay on an earth that is filled with abuse, pain, and horrible events, that God would show me what I was here to really do. My Divine-Self was communicating with God, but my human self was drowning in this darkness that was palpable. Yet, something deep within me reached out and called my neighbor.

In all of the miracles of my life, this miracle—that my neighbor was home at that exact day and that exact time and picked up her phone—is the greatest. Because she came and sat with me in the darkest moment of my life is the reason that I am still here.

After minutes, hours—time that I was not truly aware of—of me laying on the floor of my office with my neighbor sitting beside me, it was time for me to pick up my daughter from pre-school. At the moment, I was barely coherent, feeling as through I had just escaped the jaws of hell, as I had just walked through the most intense river of pain. But I had made the decision to stay, so life would resume.

Little did I know that life would never be the same. The old Keira had died that day. Through the excruciating pain that had moved through me, the old version of myself had died. And like all great alchemists, I had been made new through the light of God. It all began in my experience driving over to pick my daughter up from school.

The visions began to return as I was driving to the pre-school. After 18 months of pure silence from God, the receptive waves had been once again been opened, and they would prove to get stronger and stronger from this moment on.

The vision of a scripture story I had been raised with was shown to me as a drove. I saw it like I was actually there. It was the story of a prophet in jail. It was the story of Joseph Smith, sitting crouched in the corner of the dingiest, dirtiest jail, asking God, "O God, where art thou? And where is the pavilion that covereth thy hiding place?"

I saw and knew exactly how he felt. I had just been screaming those words as I was moving through my hell. Where was God? And why did it feel like He was hiding from me? But in this vision, I also heard God say in response to Joseph, "My son, peace be unto thy soul; thine adversity and thine afflictions shall be but a small moment."

I felt that this vision was for me. This was a message of truth—that this moment would be a small moment in time. And then I heard God say, "Keira, this will all be for your good."

Driving down the road, feeling exhausted, numb, worn out, and depleted, I could've never imagined this experience being for my good. And yet, I now see that God was correct. This experience would change my life for the better. **I would be a different person because of this pain.** I would truly rise in my purpose and my gifts because of this experience.

God had answered my prayers, just not in the way I would've ever imagined my prayers being answered.

My connection with the Divine only grew from then on. I was taught through metaphors, parables, stories, dreams, and visions regularly. I began creating a sacred space in my home where I would go every morning to connect to God and to my higher self. I believe that this is what kept the lines of communication open between me and the Divine. Each morning, I would wake up early, sit on the ground of my office, and **ask.** As I did so, I was inspired to write my first book, "The Hidden Gifts Within the Trauma of Sexual Abuse."

The process of writing this book was sacred, powerful, and solidified my connection to receiving from the Divine.

On the morning I had set to be the day this book would be published; I woke up early and went to my sacred space. The darkness had come and, once again, was seeping into my mind. I didn't want to go through with it. The fears, the doubt, the uncertainty… it was all too much. *Who was I to write this book?* The darkness began to get heavier and heavier. It felt like a weighted blanket being forced onto my body, and I just wanted to give in and quit. That is when I decided to go into a self-love meditation I had been practicing. I went into this meditation with a deep sincere prayer, begging to be released from this darkness and to see my next step.

I was shown a vision of myself standing in the middle of the stars. Everywhere I looked there were stars and, out in the distant, a beautiful woman was coming towards me. Soon I saw her face, yet it was my face, but far more beautiful. As she came close to me, the love that radiated from her enveloped me. At first, I thought that *this must be my higher self, and she must be coming to help me through this challenging moment.* But when this woman took me into her arms, and held me to her chest, I remembered Her. It was my Mother. My Divine Mother.

The love that She had for me healed me instantly. It was if I was made new within Her love and Her presence. I asked Her why she looked like me, and she replied: "Because I am in you, as you are in me." This moment in time lasted for what felt like hours. I soaked up Her sacred love and, when this vision left me, I knew that I would have the strength to publish my book. I knew that I could do anything in this world because of Her love.

And so, it was. I published my book with ease and never looked back. Divine creation became the theme song to my life. I would receive a vision, a dream, or an intuitive thought, and I would begin moving forward with creation. I was guided to create Freedom House Publishing Co. with no prior experience in publishing. I have watched the Divine teach me how to create systems and programs to support that company to be successful. I created digital courses, podcasts, coaching programs, and mastermind groups and soon to be Centers of Hope, designed after this manner: **receiving from the Divine, taking action, and watching miracles occur**.

This is not to say that life is easy all the time. I always encounter darkness as I step into new and bigger callings, every single time. But now I can move through the darkness much faster and easier.

I have learned that I am truly not alone. I have learned that I can ask for support in any way possible. In my darkest times I have reached out and asked for Christ to come and lay His hands on my head and bless me. I cannot see Him, but I feel the distinct difference in my body, my mind, and my soul afterwards. I have come to learn that I can work with Christ in a partnership—asking Him to help me heal and supporting me in my transitions to make me new.

I also reach out for extra support from the Divine Mother. I often ask Her to come and place Her hands on my heart to ease the pain that I may be feeling. I ask for Her golden, liquid love to pour over and through me to ease my pain, to heal and fill in the gaps within my energy fields, and to activate my own light.

And, of course, my team of angels—they are a crucial piece to my everyday life. Each morning I call them all in by saying, "I call in all of my angels, my guides, my leaders, my teachers, my healers, my protectors, and any ascended masters who have been assigned to me in and through the light of Christ," and then I give them assignments. So, if am needing help with raising my children, I ask for support there. If I am wanting to bring two more women into my mastermind group, I ask them to find the perfect fit women who need my work. To write this chapter, I asked them to hold the space and time so I could sit in silence and complete the chapter with ease. I often ask them to hold open an hour for me to podcast in silence (which is tricky with five kids and a few at home for homeschooling). Yet, they show up each time with miracles and pathways opened.

I want to clarify that I do not see them with my physical eyes. I often don't even feel them. But I have daily proof that when I ask for their support with distinct assignments, they show up every single time and give support where needed. When I am needing extra love, comfort, and guidance, they do communicate with me through numbers. I will see 222 or 444 or any set of 3 consecutive numbers on a consistent basis. It is like a little love note being passed in class, but instead it is a message being passed from the spiritual world to the physical world—from my angels to me.

In a world where loneliness, depression, anxiety and suicide rates are at an all-time high, this information is so deeply important. It tells us that we are not alone; that we have access to the Source of all life form. And, not only do we have access, but we can collaborate and communicate with God as well. God is the Source for me, and I find so much joy in my connection with God and my whole spiritual team. God, the Divine Mother, Christ, and my angels are my stable floor in a world with crumbling foundations and walls that seem to be made out of paper.

There are many more stories that I would love to share, but I want to finish this chapter with the story on how and why it was in my highest good that God pulled my dream house on land out from under my feet, after leading me towards it for months. I feel that sharing this story is so important because *our time is not God's time.* Often, if we do not receive the answer, we are looking for at the time we are seeking, we usually fall into the default of doubt. It is then easy to wonder if God is real, and if He even cares about us when our prayers are not answered the way we want them to be.

In 2015, we sold our home on June 13th, the day God had told me we would sell it. We moved out the end of June into my parents' house, like I mentioned earlier. After 14 months, we moved into a beautiful home that was bigger and greater than I had ever dreamed of. But it never felt like mine. I remember when we were designing it, I had the impression to *build it to sell*. So, we designed it with the most beautiful flooring, counters, cabinets, etc. It felt like a holding place. Life got hard in this house. This was the home where my memories of trauma surfaced. It was in this home that we faced the hardest financial struggles of our lives. Our four years in this home was intense and heavy.

In January of 2020, my husband and I decided that we would be making the move to Idaho in the summer; a dream he had created years earlier. He moved to Utah to learn a certain type of real estate, while I stayed in Arizona with our five kids. But the pandemic hit while he was gone, so homeschooling 5 kids began, and life got even more intense for me. We decided to forgo our plans of waiting until the summer to move since the kids weren't in school anymore, Dan came home and we got the house ready to sell in just a month.

I'll always remember when we had a relator look at our home before we listed. He let us know it could be very hard to sell our house since COVID-19 had just hit. I told him that I would pray, and he jokingly said, "I think God's answering machine is probably pretty full right now." That's when I looked at him and said, "God is guiding this move—our house will sell within the first weekend." We listed our house and drove up to Idaho to find our new one.

My lifelong dream was to live on acreage. I wanted space. I wanted nature. And that is why I wanted the house in Arizona that we lost. It wasn't my real dream, but it was close enough. I now see that God had taken that house away, not because He was being mean, but so He could give me my true dream later.

We got to Idaho and had four cities where we wanted to look at homes. We were unsure of which city to move to, so we had multiple houses to look at. On the day we had set to look at homes, I asked my angels to show us which house we were to buy and what city would be the best option. Immediately, all the houses in every city except for Middleton were taken off the market that morning. And that's when I knew we were being led to the small town of Middleton.

There were three houses available, and one was a perfect fit. But no matter how many times I walked through it and prayed—this house was not it. I was feeling so frustrated and overwhelmed. Why weren't we being led? We went to the skate park to let the kids skate and to talk about the houses. At that moment, my sister texted me an address in Middleton. It was a house that just went on the market. It was much smaller than what we were looking for, but everything inside of me told me to go. So, we called our relator, jumped in the van, and drove to a house that seemed to be hidden. *That is one of my checklist dreams; to live in a house that is hard to find and tucked away in peace.*

We drove up to this tiny house in the middle of the wildest two acres. I stepped my foot on the land and it felt like lightening had shot up my body. I knew this land was mine, even though it was covered in wild bushes, weeds up to our waists, and not one tree. But it was mine. I could feel it. We walked out back and saw the most beautiful view of the mountains. My heart sung with joy and tears rolled down my cheeks. I knew God had prepared this home for me. He had pulled away the other home because He had something so much better waiting. It just took five years for us to be ready for it. I said, "Yes, let's make an offer!"

But our current house in Arizona had just been listed one day before. We had to wait to see if we could get an offer. And seeing that many homes in our neighborhood weren't selling, we needed to wait.

The next day I told my husband that we needed to make an offer. This home was to be ours. At that exact moment, our Arizona realtor called with surprise and joy to tell us our home had sold—full price and on the first weekend! We prayed out of joy and called our Idaho relator to tell him we wanted to make an offer. He called back five minutes later and told us the house had sold five minutes before we called.

I was devasted. I was confused. God had told me in every way that this house would be ours. So why didn't He hold it for five minutes?

We stopped by a restaurant so I could run in and grab a sandwich. I was in line, praying and asking my angels to please move the obstacles around so that we could get this house. I was asking for clarity and comfort. A I ordered my food; the total was $11.11. And at that moment, I knew that everything was going to be okay. I jumped in the car feeling so much peace and told Dan, *"this will all work out, my angels are working on it, and we don't need to worry."*

From that moment on, faith became the only ground we stood on.

We made an offer on the perfect fit house in Middleton that didn't feel right, but was now the only option, and our offer was denied. There were no other homes to choose from, and our Arizona home was set to close in 30 days. But my angels had told me it was all taken care of.

A few days later, we were at our friend's cabin in Wyoming. I had been praying for guidance and direction. That morning, I woke up and outside our cabin was a moose with 4 white legs. I looked at Dan and told him that this was an omen. Our answer would come today. *Why did I think that?* I have no idea, except that this moose seemed special and, when I saw it, those words came to my mind. God speaks to us in any way that we are willing to receive.

That day we had our answer. Our relator called and let us know that the offer fell through on the house in Idaho! My sacred land was now available. We quickly made an offer and the road to this dream was now becoming a reality. My angels had come to tell me that day at the sandwich shop through angel numbers that all was taken care of, *and it was.*

But this was only the first step to getting this house. The rest of the journey would require more faith than I had ever exercised before. Getting the loan after years of financial struggle was hard. Add to it that we were both self-employed and it got even harder. And then add COVID to it… getting loans was nearly impossible. On May 28th, our Arizona house closed, so we packed our 12-seater van to the brim, and drove it, along with a moving truck, to Idaho without a home to move into.

A week before we left for Idaho, I had been in my sacred space praying and asking God to please let our loan close so we could move directly into our Idaho home when we arrived. I was shown the vision of Moses and Red Sea—that miraculous story when Moses led the Israelites to the edge of the Red Sea with Pharaoh and his army at their tail. The Red Sea didn't part, miles before they reached it. No, it parted the moment they arrived. At the very last moment. Then God said to me, "This is your Red Sea. It will part at the last moment."

This was all that God was giving me. An invitation to trust harder than I ever have before and believe that the loan would close.

The whole drive to Idaho I spoke this truth. *"My Red Sea will part. This loan will close. We will get this house."*

Our close date came and went without the loan closing. The sellers gave us an extension, and we arrived in Idaho homeless. Luckily the sellers didn't live at the home we were buying, so they allowed us to park our U-Haul in front of the house while we lived in my brother's house for a few days. A day turned into a week, and we got another extension.

Our family and loved ones were telling us to start looking for rental houses. But I was reading Florence Scovel Shinn's work and her words were loud in my heart. She teaches that if you want to manifest something, your mind and heart must match. I couldn't want to move into the house and then allow my mind to look for rentals. They had to match. So, I didn't look for a rental house. I prayed each day that God would pour miracles over our loan and that we would get the house in the perfect way. And that week extended to another week.

We found an Airbnb that was in someone's basement, with the kitchen sink next to the washer and dryer. It felt depressing and dark and it was hard to keep the faith while we were there. The second week passed and still no luck. We got another extension and, with the inspiration from my brother, we decided to make the most out of our time without a home and went up to the magical mountain town of McCall, Idaho. Each morning in my sacred space, I would sit in the middle of an aspen grove and a deer would show up and look me right in the eyes. It felt like a nudge of hope. A simple reminder that all would work out.

But still, another few days went by, and we were running out of money with all of these Airbnb's. I reached out to my best friend from high school, Kendra Kellis, who had also recently to Idaho. I hadn't talked to her in over a decade, but I was desperate. I asked her if we could stay with her for a few days. She opened her home and her heart to our family and the reconnection was beautiful and healing at a time of such uncertainly.

It had now been 3 weeks and the sellers would not extend anymore. I was feeling a lot of anger towards the people working on the loan. I kept thinking, "Don't they care that we have been homeless for 3 weeks?" I was praying that night, asking God why he hadn't worked the miracle yet. I was asking why He had strung me along *again*. I was so afraid that the same thing was going to happen again, and I'd have my dream home ripped out from underneath me at the last minute.

But then God showed me these people's lives who were working on the loan. He showed me their struggles and what they were going through. I was then invited to pray for them. Not just a two second prayer, but a deep and meaningful prayer. I was invited to pray for each one of their struggles and to pray for their lives. Once I had done this, the anger left me, and I fully turned everything over to God. Tomorrow was the last day we could get this house, and I had surrendered the results. We woke up with a message that our loan had closed! We had the time and date of when we would be signing the loan documents and the keys would be ours.

I cried out of joy. I cried out of wonder. God's words had held true. The Red Sea had parted at the very last moment. *God delivered.*

I will always remember the joy that it was to run through our land, knowing that this sacred land would be ours. I also remember the joy I felt knowing that God hadn't strung me along five years ago and then left me. No, God had a larger plan. We would've never been able to buy the Idaho home without the money we made from the Arizona home. That home was a crucial piece to me getting this sacred land. God had lined it all up perfectly. It just wasn't in my time; it was God's time.

We have now been in this home for 18 months and have planted over 80 trees. I have my own sacred aspen grove that overlooks the mountain range where I go to pray and have sacred space. I have the absolute privilege of watching the sunrise over the mountains every single morning. I feel God's presence as I see the brilliance of the sun appear and warm the earth. I love listening to all of the animals greet the sun as it peeks its brilliant head over the mountains. The chorus of moos from the cows, the roosters singing their morning songs, and the dogs saying hello to the morning are one of the many joys I receive from living on this land.

What I have learned through these past seven years is that God is always waiting for us. It is never that He is waiting for us to be perfect, special or holy. No, He is waiting for us to be opened to receive Him. I have learned that Christ is here, always with His arms open, waiting for us to come to Him. We are the ones that hold back the Divine. We are the dam that pushes away the miracles. If we want to truly connect and partner with the Divine, then it is up to us. All we have to do is lower our guard, open our hearts, and ask.

We must ask to receive and then take action on what is given.

This method has been taught in thousands of different ways by so many prophets of old, ascended masters, and thought leaders. It is not new information. It is the wisest information that has come to this earth.

If you ask and then step forward with faith, the miracles that are ready for you will be greater than you could've ever imagined. You are ready now, just as you are to receive.

It is time to step forward.

What insights, inspiration, and ideas came to you while you read this chapter? Make some notes below:

_____

_____

_____

_____

_____

_____

_____

_____

_____

_____

_____

_____

_____

_____

_____

_____

_____

_____

_____

_____

Chapter 14
SPIRITUAL TEAMWORK
By: Hollie Warnick

I've come a long way, and
I've got a long way to go.

I've been making deals with the Divine for ages. That's usually how we do things. I would study up, ask something, and wait for God to say something. As a young child, I sometimes waited for a thunderous voice to break out from the clouds and tell me exactly what to do. As in: "HOLLIE, THIS IS GOD—THE GOOD GUY GOD. DO THIS THING NOW!" and then I would do the dang thing and life would be roses.

Not so. Not how it happened for me—ever. I always had to make my decision first. I had to take an action, try something, or make a move. Only then would I receive the go ahead or the "go back!" I felt I needed to hear.

I grew up practicing a very structured religion that was heavily enmeshed with my family and the community in which I lived. I didn't always follow what I was taught in church, but I really tried. I was told who the Divine was—from age, gender, and voice to dislikes and manner of dressing. God from a dating app, I guess. For a long time, I took what I thought was my religion's word for how I should do life and I made it my playbook. When life was happy and quaint, it was because I was following my good girl checklist. When life was sad and dark, it was because there was some rule I didn't follow.

I often doled out my personal authority and power to religion. This left me irresponsible for anything that went on in my life. Because I had handed over my agency to some other entity, I did little exploring on my own. Any exploring that I did do left me feeling ashamed and guilty. After years of struggling in dark despair, with highs in between, I finally did some healing work that transformed my old way of being. I no longer had to depend on my religion to tell me what was right or wrong or how to live. Slowly, I stretched out of my comfort zone to learn about other religions, philosophies, and teachings. This was so satisfying to my very curious mind. It had become okay to venture out on my own and discover new ways to be.

Still, in the back of my mind, a voice would pipe up and say, "That's a sin! You're a sinner!" I would even get people around me to reflect that message back to me, so we could all condemn my actions together. These verdicts were debilitating at times, and boosted me forward at others. I remember a friend being upset that a few of us were praying over our meal despite having consumed alcohol. I thought, *"How silly that he thinks we can't pray to God because we've had alcohol."* I also remember getting in trouble with the law often, so I could prove I was a bad person. But guess what? God speaks to all who listen, even the bad or "unworthy" ones.

Maybe some would still argue that I am not worthy to speak to God, but if that's how their God is, I'll follow a different, more accepting and loving God, thank you very much. The Divine speaks to me as well as to those walking down the street yelling obscenities.

The top question here is, how do I hear the Divine? I used to limit it to just after my prayer. I was taught a very specific way to pray to God and to then listen after all that praying. I was to be quiet and still after the benediction. I heard many songs about "the still, small voice" of the Spirit communicating to my heart. This was a little tough, because I didn't often have awe-inspiring insights right after my prayer. I love the idea, but in practice, this wasn't a common occurrence for me. So, God and I came up with our own way to work together. And, quite frankly, I think we both agree that it works better for us!

Back in the day, God and I used to make deals, like a swap. When I was in elementary, I knew—*knew*—my life would be better if I had this very specific purse from Target. It was a black, long-strapped, saddle bag kind of deal. The amazing soft plastic had stars embossed on the flap. So cool! This purse was going to change my life. I was going to be more confident, more popular, and more stylish. What more could a tween need?

My mother had said no at the store. I was afraid it would be gone the next time we went back and I was desperate for it. I needed that purse badly. And whom do you ask when your parents say no? God.

Dear God, I pleaded from my knees, *please, please, please let me have that purse! I promise I'll be good and participate at church. I'll do better at reading my scriptures. I'll pray more! I'll be a better person. I won't have bad thoughts. I'll do everything my parents ask. Just please, please let me have that purse! I'll be so good if you just let me have that purse.* In my mind, this purse was the key to happiness and I anxiously wanted God to deliver. I would probably never make it if I didn't have that purse. I understood it to be my salvation.

Well, God did deliver. I got that purse. It was cute and trendy. It did not make me more popular. Reading my scriptures more didn't last long. I was incapable of not having any "bad" thoughts. In fact, life wasn't much different for me having that purse. Sometimes when we get exactly what we ask for, it isn't the answer to our problems. You may be thinking, that's a great lesson to learn at 10, but how does that help me better commune with the Divine? Let me tell another story.

In my teenage years, life and relationship tensions became overwhelming. I turned in many different directions, seeking reprieve from the turmoil and discord I felt inside and out. In an hour of desperation, I struck another deal with God. *Dear God, could you make me never have existed? Please, please, I'm begging. Take me out of this life. Make it so no one remembers or misses me. I know I can't commit suicide, so just end it this way, please! If I didn't exist, then no one would be sad or affected by me not being here. I don't even want another chance, just disappear me. Then I won't remember me either. Don't just end my earth life—end my soul, please God, please! I never want to have existed.* I wept, I pleaded, I cried, I scraped, I clawed and I heard nothing.

I didn't hear a yes, a no, or anything at all. No opinions or options were brought up and I listened really hard here, ladies and gentlemen. Why was mum the word on this super important, life-altering request? Why would God ignore me in my greatest hour of need? Radio silence? *Really?*

God was quiet. He didn't send anyone into my basement room to ease my pain. I was alone, exhausted, huddled on my floor. It was just me as far as I could tell. I let my sorrow and grief towards life leak out. I was emptying a long-held storage of despair.

In that interminable silence, I discovered I felt better. The unbearable thought that I shouldn't exist slowly drained away. I was somehow more at ease and peace. I knew God would not meet my demands. Inexplicably, the deafening quiet reassured me. God wasn't ready to take me out. Maybe I wasn't damned after all. Maybe I could continue in life as it was.

Looking back, some could proclaim God was there and I just wasn't listening. Maybe some would argue that this is proof that God doesn't exist. But when I reflect on this event, I think the Divine and all my Spiritual Attendants were there. I imagine they listened diligently without judgment or advice. I presume they all supported me, regardless of what I expressed. I even suppose that their witnessing my lamentations was the true gift. I think the therapeutic process of expression was a saving grace for me at that time. Not being bailed out of my drama and trauma by some rescuer was a lesson for my Soul. Despite future depressive dips and paradigm-shattering events, I found that life wasn't so excruciating after that. I found that life was going to keep me and I was going to keep it.

In my early years, I had heard of another way to work with God. It was to go ahead and do something and ask God to give you this "stupor of thought" if it was the wrong action. I went with it. I have to say that the only real stupor of thought I experienced was doubt, fear, and shame about my actions. *Was that from God?* I wondered. *Or am I just working myself up from being outside my comfort zone?*

Taking a step in any direction seemed complicated. I felt frozen in the fear of what would come from choosing. Often, I wouldn't make any decision, which turned out to be a choice of its own. Making a selection filled me with anxiety and worry that I was doing it wrong. I was constantly evaluating my actions as right or wrong. I wasn't sure this stupor of thought was a good exercise because I frequently felt so insecure in my selections.

Luckily, I was beginning to wake up. I was starting to see how taking action wasn't supposed to be perfect every time. I noticed that God wasn't condemning me for making wrong moves. I wasn't being penalized for failing. I didn't hear any reprimands from on high. There was no fire or brimstone to reprove my actions. God wasn't even correcting me. All these concepts I thought were the tools of God (chastisement, punishment, guilt, failure, right and wrong) were not! Lo and behold, God was still there when I messed up. The Divine still showed face when I stayed up late or didn't make it to my church meetings. No matter what I wore or said, God still spoke to me. Whenever I truly reached out, there was a spark of love waiting. I didn't always feel it, but I finally had the conviction that God would love me no matter what I did. I'm so happy I've gotten this message at last. Now, I can share it with others.

Speaking of sharing, I am now the mother of 4 young children. Children don't always like sharing. Children are messy. Children don't always follow the rules and they don't do perfect. They're great teachers. I'm joyful to know now that perfect is the mess. Perfect is trial and error. Everything I do is exactly what I'm meant to do. Life is unfolding precisely as it should. This is the mercy I get to reveal to my children and others—to you. Feel and know that you are under Divine protection and enfolded in the loving arms of the Divine as you move through life, whichever path you take.

On our individual life path, we can allow ourselves to work with Spirit in numerous ways. I hope you're more ready than ever to choose despite the fear of the future. I did mention that I actually have a specific, constructive process through which I commune with the Divine. As I boldly step forward on each of my endeavors, I check in with Spirit. Let's do one more short story to really illustrate what the process looks and feels like.

When I was away at university, I ended up meeting the man I would marry. I knew it early on, but not before a friend realized something was up.

"Who is this Rob guy?" he asked.

"Just a guy I'm dating," I placidly responded. No big deal.

But that got me thinking that maybe this guy *was* a big deal. There was a different feel in our relationship and I knew that I could marry this man. I resigned myself that I would marry him and, just to make sure I was following all the rules, I decided I better tell God about marrying him. I pushed the information through in a short walking prayer and heard the response, "Don't pass him up." Plain and simple. Nothing more, nothing less: don't pass him up. I have always remembered those words and I am so glad I checked in. I had reached my verdict already, but those words set it in stone. I would not pass him up. I have continuously been surprised and rewarded for heeding this advice.

In this scenario, I had come to a conclusion that I would do a deed. It wasn't getting a material thing that would make me happier. It wasn't a task I needed God to do for me. It was a relationship *I* was building. I was firm in my direction. I was completing tasks. I took action and *then* I checked in with God. And that's how we still do it to this day. I get an inspiration and go for it. When I check in with the Divine, it's like a cheerleader egging me on. Go for it! You got this! Let's see what we can learn.

Alright, that's all fine and dandy when it comes to decision making in the moment and jumping in feet first. Now I want to share how I connect daily with the Divine.

First off, my relationship with God had to evolve. It was just one guy who, much like my own father, wasn't super talkative and was pretty hands off. There wasn't a lot of touchy-feely emotion between us. God was aloof and far away. I desired more hands on, involved nurturing. Enter "Spiritual Team." I'd been hearing these terms for a long while and I had been working with Christ for decades, but the team was basically just Christ. It felt a bit lonely. It was time to let the other Spirits in!

I grew up in fear of negative entities crowding in and taking over my life and body. If truth be told, these beliefs kept me in the dark for a long time. I didn't feel safe reaching out to any being besides Christ. I trusted only Christ. Still, I felt that there was more available and more out there to receive. Why would God be so limited? In the past, I had studied a sundry of philosophies and religions. Was it finally time for me to let them in? Was it time to expand my version of the Divine?

I began, little by little, to invite other teachings, energies, and Spirits in *through Christ only* (I was being very vigilant). Because of my invitation, many showed up. Ancestors, Ascended Masters, crystal energy, plant medicine, passed on family members, shamans, and guides all arrived as I was willing to receive them. In some cases, I was uncomfortable. In others, I was elated. How could I have been missing out on this for so long? I think we each get to develop our own relationship with the Divine. To me, the Divine is so much more inclusive.

I'm building relationships all the time with my True Self, my husband, my kids, my creations, and the Divine. It's taken the removal and deletion of old paradigms. I've erased or accepted what before seemed a paradox. My eyes have opened to a much more expansive world that not only includes one Creator, but a myriad of advocates on my spiritual team. I'm not alone ever, and neither are you. Even in my darkest hours, I truly feel my team is here for me. Whether it's an ancestor, Buddha himself, or all of the above, I now feel and experience Divine encouragement throughout my day—not just after a perfect prayer.

One very special relationship has recently opened up to me. It's growing little by little. It's finally safe to develop a relationship with the Divine Mother. A woman. A loving, giving, nurturing, patient female who holds me when I need it. She lets me cry in her lap and doesn't judge. She doesn't advise or project, she just hears and acknowledges each of us. What a gift. What an infinite treasure for me. It's still opening up for me. It's been hard to trust, but I'm getting there.

I invite you to start trusting your Divine Spiritual Team. Invite them to pull up a seat at your table, even if you have to add the stipulation "only through light and truth." Let them support and guide your path. The more you invite them to do in your space and place, the more they *will* do in your life. They respect your boundaries. Allow them to hold the way open as you follow your inspirations. Ask them questions. Get to know them. Get to know yourself. Give yourself permission to connect to other realms of light. They are there whether we access them or not.

Furthermore, I request that you not condemn yourself. I invite you to try new things, to look further, and crest the horizon without knowing what exactly is next. Leave the judgment and disapproval out of it. Love yourself forward and backward, inside and out. What would life be like if I had not denounced myself for all my actions? I consider these bygone events to have been integral to my growth. What would the world be like if God had granted my wish to exit life or he hadn't agreed upon my betrothal? The real question is, what would have happened if I hadn't gotten that purse?! I'm kidding.

Although I cannot change my past, I can change how I feel about my past. I can leave it there and leave it with God. I can choose to feel the love and support immediately as I work with the Divine. I entreat you to do the same. Experience the Divine in *your* way. Allow your Spirit to fly alongside your Spiritual team. They will guide and direct your efforts towards your highest potential.

What insights, inspiration, and ideas came to you while you read this chapter? Make some notes below:

_____

_____

_____

_____

_____

_____

_____

_____

_____

_____

_____

_____

_____

_____

_____

_____

_____

_____

_____

_____

Chapter 15

TEAMWORK BRINGS THE DREAMS FORTH

By: Randa Stratton-Dutcher

I am a mother of five children, wife to my high school sweetheart (twice), singer, songwriter, cowgirl, self-proclaimed poet, baker, and connoisseur of pillows and French toast. As a 5th generation native, I am an Arizona girl through and through—born and raised here in the Southwest. They say that makes me a unicorn in this day and age.

I grew up a member of The Church of Jesus Christ of Latter-Day Saints, which I still attend. There I learned about Deity, scripture, the importance of family, and many more wonderful things. I am currently unraveling culture and old traditions and beliefs to find light and truth. I find that my relationship with God and Christ ever deepen as I seek to fulfill my purpose and use the gifts, They gave me.

My parents both grew up on ranches in a small town, instilling in me a love of horses that brings me a great sense of joy and confidence. I was 5 years old and had just started kindergarten when my brother was born. My parents got divorced and we moved several times after that. My dad lived far away from us while attending school and working. We (my mom and brother) lived with my grandparents, aunts, and uncles while my mom went to school and worked until she remarried. It was an adventure; I grew up quickly and became a professional people pleaser. The benefits outweighed the bad though, as I now have a deep connection with my extended family because I lived with so many of them. I lived in a few different places and learned how to make new friends quickly. Not to mention the extra love and support we received because of our situation.

They say you can't relive the past, but this is a lie. I buried my feelings from my childhood, but relived it over and over as I set up relationships for failure. I had to win at everything; I had to make everyone else lose. This made for a rocky marriage as I tried to balance pleasing people with being right all the time. Burying the past feelings and experiences I had hurt me and all of my relationships. As I unexpectedly became pregnant with my 5th child, my marriage fell apart. We separated and eventually divorced, making us both single parents. I knew how it would all go and how we could co-parent—splitting weekends and holidays just as my parents did with me and my brother. I wouldn't try to get along. I would be angry and bitter, because that is what divorce is supposed to "look like." Right?

What I didn't know is that my childhood experiences didn't have to be my experiences now. I could actually have a say in how it went. Two and a half years later, my ex-husband and I got back together. With counseling and other avenues of healing, we remarried and are very happy and in love. Relationships take time, work, and healing no matter the circumstance. He and I continue to do our work—for prevention is always better than medicine!

Through the healing I learned and experienced during my divorce, I learned I had spiritual gifts. Through the pain and sorrow of my family being broken, I relied more upon God. I gave him my heart and he showed me how strong I could be. He showed me how to use my gifts and assisted me in healing myself, my marriage, and my family. I felt very literally stripped of all of my ego, pride, and "things" I had thought were important as God led me through that deeply painful time. Now I assist others in doing the same—letting go of the past so that the future can be created from possibility instead of pain, fear, and sabotage.

Have you ever been inspired to do something, be something, say something, or create something that seemed big and exciting, yet you have zero clue how to accomplish it? In that moment of inspiration, it feels so real, so possible, and so exciting that it propels you forward. That all-encompassing feeling stays with you until, well... it doesn't. For me, this has been a ceiling I butt up against for most of my life. I am a creator. I feel inspired and hear whisperings of creation, music, books, and ideas that are exciting and fun and full of possibility. Often, the excited feelings get me to a certain point and then the unknown shows up. How do I get past this point?

Full disclosure... sometimes I don't get past it. Sometimes I take myself out of the running. But when I *do* get past the self-sabotaging and uncertainty, it takes the help of a higher power.

From a young age, I always knew there was a higher power. I was taught these things, but I also knew and experienced it for myself. I learned songs about God, Christ, and Angels and I always felt so peaceful and happy as I sang them. I suppose music is where I first learned to team up with the Divine and use power to transcend my humanity into art that could touch the hearts and minds of others.

My higher power is God, Christ, Heavenly Mother, and Angels. When I allow these beings to lead me into what sometimes feels like the dark (because it's the unknown and that can be scary), miracles always occur. This blind faith of saying yes to being led by the beings that can see the whole, infinite picture is Divine Collaboration. It's the land of "I don't know that I don't know." It takes faith and courage to take the first step and then to keep taking steps towards the highest purpose of my being, for that is where I am being led in those moments. I am led to an unknown dimension and version of myself that I feel is possible but is not in my reality yet. There will be doubts, fears, growth, and it will be uncomfortable, but when you say yes, you will be transformed into someone who has been led by Divine hands.

Whenever I sing, I ask that concourses of Angels sing with me. I ask that they buffer any human mistakes I might make and help every heart listening to this song to know and feel God's love for them and the truthfulness of whatever message the lyrics bring—whether it's "The Star-Spangled Banner" or a lullaby. When I say this prayer and collaborate with God, it works.

As an adult, I still knew there were beings of light; I still felt peace and joy when singing. But I let myself believe that I couldn't use any of my gifts unless they were related to my family or church. I buried my talents and shut down the creative part of myself so I could focus on church and family. God didn't ask me to do that—no one told me to do that—but it was the reality I made up. The more I shut down, the worse my marriage got. I focused on the flaws of my spouse and children. I tried focusing on fitness and being in shape, doing the activities he liked, and being with people he wanted to be with to "make my husband happy." But, in reality, I was just ensuring I would stay unhappy because I wasn't focusing on my divine connection with God—my maker, creator, and a being who loves me and knows me infinitely and eternally better than I know myself.

That's when God used my divorce as an opportunity to show me who I really was. It was in small, simple ways, but he placed Angels in my path to pull me from the shadows. I began singing again. My friend, Joyce Brinton, taught vision board classes and invited me along to tell my story and share how a vision board changed my life. Then I would sing a few songs. I even learned to play guitar! I became a certified Muscle Tester and Energy Healer and still use these certifications in my coaching.

After I remarried my husband, I let myself go back to complacency and the deep darkness of suicide ideation. I think we all have some sort of habit or cycle we habitually run into during the course of our lives. Remarriage wasn't easy, and we still had a lot of learning and healing to do. I am still working on overcoming the cycle of "when it gets hard, I shut down, want to be right, make others wrong, and people please."

Once again, I was reminded that, when I say no to the inspirations whispered to me, they become dead weights that drag me further and further until I release them or I implode. I think it would be a lot easier if I just released them to begin with, instead of resisting, but I'm still learning.

I eventually hired a coach, as I wanted to write a book about my divorce and remarriage. It felt so right. It felt like God was calling me to do it. Many people have reached out to us and asked us to share how we were able to reconcile. I wanted to share the message of hope with the world. I began writing a book with my coach and using the tools I had learned thus far, coupled with tools of inviting God to write with me, has been nothing short of miraculous. When I partner with God, I feel this sort of buzzing all around me and things come to mind that are not of myself.

Once I said yes, a lot of other creations came to the surface as well. A digital course in forgiveness, another digital course on sabotage. My podcast is the "Going Dutch" podcast. Music has been written and recorded. I have held two women's retreats, assisting them to reignite the light that has been dimmed by shutting down, shutting it out, or just forgetting how to keep it lit. Each creation has been scary, each time I've wanted to quit, and each time the darkness has felt too strong to overcome. The darkness wants us to shut down, to relive the past over and over so life looks hopeless, miserable, and without possibility.

The truth is, however, that it doesn't matter how many times you fall down, dip back into past ways or cycles, or sabotage yourself as long as you get back up again and again. God is always there to lift you up and remind you that you are not wasted space and you're not alone. You belong to the Divine, and you are always, always, always worthy of love, life, joy, peace, contentment, fun, and—most of all— God's help.

What insights, inspiration, and ideas came to you while you read this chapter? Make some notes below:

Chapter 16

DANCING WITH THE DIVINE

By: Jessica Tietjen, J.D.

It can be cool in the shade of the early morning before the sun comes up. But we know the sun will always rise and with it the light and warmth, the growth and nutrients, the day and ultimately the night again. So too is the Divine Mother – always there even in the dark, cold times we know she will rise again soon. We need only look inside and wait for her presence and guidance. We need only to turn on the music of life inside our souls to dance with the Divine.

My History with God and the Divine

Thus far in my life, my dance with the Divine has been inconsistent at best. As the granddaughter of the well-known Rev. Dr. John H. Tietjen, I was raised a good Lutheran girl, required to sit in the front row of church every Sunday morning. During my childhood and teenage years, I had tremendous moments dancing with the Divine but failed to fully see and appreciate their unique beauty, given my level of understanding at the time. I grew to doubt my own recollection and experiences as they felt like that of fictional stories rather than reality. As I grew into adulthood, I attended college, grad school, and law school—gaining lots of knowledge but little related to God or the Divine. I never strayed far from my faith—always remaining steadfast in my belief of God, Christ, and the Holy Spirit. But I also always kept my distance—never allowing what I intuitively knew existed below the surface to truly take shape or come into existence.

I briefly considered following in the footsteps of my grandfather but choose instead to pursue law and ultimately begin my career in the corporate world. I quickly grew into a leader, repeatedly expanding my responsibility to various parts of the business world.[1] At work, I met and ultimately married a good, kind, smart, and wonderful man. But a man who didn't (and still doesn't) believe in God or the Divine, which further complicated my relationship with God, my faith, and the church. I felt little of God's presence in the church of my youth and started a journey to find him in other churches. I saw glimpses of God—moments where I could hear the music—but I could never quite join the dance.

Then, after the birth of my son, I experienced a major health crisis causing me to have chronic hives, pain, and even anaphylaxis. This extreme pain and suffering, coupled with numerous tests and no clear medical answer to my issues, led me to a rock bottom I'd never experienced before. I needed my faith. I needed the Divine just to survive, to carry me through this time when I could not walk on my own, let alone dance. For when we cannot carry ourselves, God will come to carry us, but only if we ask and invite them to do so.

Renewed with the loving support of God, I was able to slowly heal both from my illness and my fragmented faith. But just as I had in the past, I kept a distance, separating myself from God just enough

---

[1] I became a leader of Legal, Human Resources/Talent Management, Information Technology, Customer Service, Marketing, Order Management, and Project Coordination.

to keep what, intuitively, I knew was required to dance with the Divine—intimacy. I knew if I got too close, if I joined the dance, I needed to be ready for what it would mean to my life. I simply wasn't ready... yet. Instead, I began to enjoy the music while avoiding the dance.

After struggling through multiple miscarriages, I discovered I was pregnant and knew immediately it was twins! I could feel both their spirits distinctly in my womb—separate, unique, and precious. This twin pregnancy was nothing like my first experience—the fear, the massive belly, the limitations, the bi-weekly doctor visits, the dozens of ultrasounds, and ultimately the C-section birth. I prayed through this pregnancy. I prayed and danced with the Divine through every beautiful, exhausting, and even disgusting moment. My beautiful babies, growing in my womb, allowed me to join the dance if even just for a short time.

I carried my twins 38 weeks when, with God's loving support, they were born healthy, able to nurse well, and spent no time in the NICU. I tandem-nursed my twin baby girls around the clock, sacrificing sleep and sanity to feed them. When the post-partum depression hit, I again needed God's loving support and tried to turn to formula for some relief from the pressure. Only then did we discover they had a food-protein intolerance (FPIES) which would prevent them from taking any formula. I cried out, "Why God?" The answer I received was, "Because you must learn you can do so much more than you think you can." And I did. I nursed those girls for 18 months, receiving divine help through the donation of milk from other mothers. I learned so much about my strength and about partnering in my dance with the Divine, to flow with the music of life rather than resist.

My twins were nine months old and my son five years old when the COVID pandemic hit. I was just starting to successfully return to work that January after I'd tried and failed numerous times prior. I was pumping during training and leadership meetings, but it was never enough. The stress of my job, combined with twins, was overwhelming. Then COVID flipped everything, for everyone, upside down.

For me, the part of the pandemic keeping us at home was the greatest gift I could have received from God. I could do my job at home with ease, taking short breaks to feed my babies or even feeding them during conference calls with no one the wiser! I had always thought I needed to be in the office to do my job but I learned a totally new way—we all did.

What a beautiful dance with the Divine the pandemic was for me. Again, I learned to go with the flow of life rather than resist. I learned to slow down, to see the beauty, and to be present with my children. I learned dancing with the Divine—seeing God up close and feeling her presence and direction—brought tremendous joy and possibility. And then, I felt divine direction to write my first book...

Writing my 1st Book – The Exceptional Life R-Evolution

When I went to write my first book, *The Exceptional Life R-Evolution,* I felt and believed the book had nothing to do with my faith, God, or anything spiritually-based at all. I just wanted to write a book and provide the insights I had discovered during the pandemic. But deep down, I knew God wanted me to write it and God had a very specific reason for doing so. Each step was guided in the most crazy and beautiful way while I allowed God to lead me through this time in my life.

Only by chance—a divinely led sequence of events[2]—did I connect with Keira Poulsen and Freedom House Publishing. Without

---

[2] I was lonely from the pandemic and wanted to meet more people. I joined Meetups and discovered a Voices of Women Summit. I decided to participate and watched Keira's session on "How to Write a Book," since I knew I was supposed to write one but had no idea how!

Keira, I am not sure I would have ever published my book and it certainly wouldn't have included the many divinely inspired sections within it! In fact, when I first met with Keira, I remember telling her, "I think there is a religious or spiritual component to this book but I am not ready to think or talk about that yet." She smiled and said, "I understand." I'm quite certain she knew, even at that early point, what God had in store for me.

I was still in denial, trying to ignore the call of the Divine and what I knew answering it would mean for my life. Subconsciously, I knew when I answered the call of the Divine, began listening to its guidance, and acting upon its direction—my whole life would change. And, ultimately, my whole life did change. It changed in the best way possible but not without pain, significant challenge, and the growth that comes from both.

I have always known God and believed in God, but I had never experienced or felt God the way I did during this journey. As I began Keira's sacred space practice[3], little by little, I started to hear a voice and receive very clear guidance and direction. I feared the voice and was even more scared of the direction and what hearing this voice would mean to my life. But, as you can imagine, the voice of God is quite persistent, and I had little choice but to keep listening to see what would happen.

During the writing of the book, I began experiencing divinely inspired moments, visions, and concepts that were clearly meant for my book. I'd watch a waterfall and clearly see the waterfall as a perfect analogy for processing the experiences in our lives. I would walk outside to get fresh air and suddenly the wildflowers were so bright, and I'd hear the words, "Wildflowers are like our thoughts," which fit perfectly in the book. One night the power went out, and so

---

[3] A sacred space is a place that has special religious or spiritual qualities, even if it's just a space in your home just for you.

came the story of challenge and darkness which leads to light and music. I even experienced divinely inspired moments that were challenging—a leader questioning how I lead—which solidified my chapter on Leadership and a "Leading Together" approach to leadership. Each vision, voice, and inspiration appeared at just the right moment and fit perfectly, helping to craft a book filled with tremendous knowledge and wisdom but written to be both relatable and enjoyable for the reader.

Just as we watch the water flow down the rocks of a waterfall, we should watch our experiences and performance. Let go of what does not serve or benefit us and continue on our journey through life, down the waterfall. Leave the moments that cause us to get stuck or unable to evolve behind and continue on, always moving forward – sometimes fast, sometimes slow, but always forward. We must never attempt to go back upstream by trying to change or redo an experience. Rather, we must observe these experiences, take them for what they are – an experience on a specific day – learn from them when possible, and then continue on in our lives.

One way to think about how our thoughts impact our lives is to think of them like wildflowers. At first, wildflowers are beautiful – there are a few here and there, with beautiful colors lighting up nature's canvas. But left to their own devices, wildflowers spread – popping up anywhere their seed lands and growing ever higher, ultimately taking over your gardens and tree beds. The flowers get taller and taller until they are as high as your hip, and you can't even pass through them.

Likewise, our thoughts start out as a useful tool, helping us process and understand our experiences. But over time, these thoughts can overtake our mind and expand as our brain thinks the same thoughts over and over and over again. Then the thoughts become overwhelming, to the point that they actually surpass the experience itself. They cast a shadow over the experience, preventing us from evolving, seeing, learning, and growing from the experience itself.

Even if I had been able to write the book on my own without these little jewels of wisdom, the divinely inspired pieces are what truly make the book so enjoyable to read. My faith in the Divine began to grow and so did my understanding of who I was hearing and what I was being asked to do next in my life. While actively writing my first book, I felt and knew there would be much more to come. For the more I danced with the Divine, the more skilled I became at dancing. As we learn, we become able to easily dance the most challenging of steps. And soon, I would be asked to dance with the Divine through a challenge I never anticipated.

God had another step for me—a critical step on my journey—to learn how to experience love in a way I had never known before. I'll stop you here; this is not a romance novel, so there is no big plot twist or secret love affair but rather the beginning of a journey to discover love of myself. Each step of the journey was placed in my path at the exact perfect moment. The first step of this new dance with the Divine was learning I would write a second book.

Really God? Another Book?

I began my second book on a family vacation (right in the middle of completing the first!) while driving to a family party. As I sat in the passenger seat of our van, with three kids screaming in the backseat, inspiration struck, and I quickly typed a message into the Notes app on my phone. I heard the words, "You must love yourself before you will make the choices that reflect this love. You know how to do it—you do it with your children. You must just learn to do it for yourself." I was shocked at receiving the beginning of a new book while still writing my first. But I knew, without a doubt in my mind, God had a plan for this next book.

My experience writing the second book has been quite different than the first—it was not a book where I had acquired years of expertise, understanding, or even background on the topic. Rather, the second book is truly a book of my journey, receiving messages from the Divine to learn about myself, to cherish myself, and to forever transform how I exist and show up in the world.

The journey and the steps I took were guided by God and provided to me in the most beautiful ways over a period of many months. With every insight, direction, and message came significant understanding, growth, and evolution of my being. God, through clear direction and instruction, provided the steps for this very special dance. Although the story of this journey is mine, the steps are meant for many.

The full story and book will be published soon, but I wanted to share a few of the most divinely inspired elements of the book. Starting with the beginning:

This is a story about a girl – a girl who wanted to belong so badly she learned to say, do, and be whatever others needed of her. She got so good at this, she forgot what she wanted, what she believed, and who she really was. She grew up only knowing herself and valuing herself through the eyes of others. Believing she was only loveable if she was loved by others. She was only worthy if others saw her worth. She was only valuable if others valued her. As a result, she never really felt she was enough – she could never feel loved, worthy, or valuable **enough**. *She was always searching for more and always longing to feel* **enough**.

The girl grew into a woman and mother, but the child seeking validation, forever wanting to be enough, lived on in her. The child always seeking her love, worth, and value from those around her and always coming up short. She could never achieve enough, be beautiful enough, or do enough. She grew exhausted, which only made things harder – harder to please, harder to maintain beauty, harder to be great at so many things – mother, wife, career, home, and more. All roles she played, yet she never even really considered the woman playing them all.

She never considered the woman always striving and never feeling good enough. Surrounded by people, yet totally alone. A smile on the face, yet pain in the heart. Successful on the surface yet lost underneath.

You see, she had not yet discovered the most transformative and important insight of life. An insight everyone needs but seems to be somewhat of a mystery – not easily found or believed. This mysterious insight is readily accessible and available to anyone – although few find and learn its value. For when we learn this insight, we finally realize our focus has been misplaced. We need not focus on others or belonging but rather on ourselves. The source of our love, worth, and value is **within** *not* **without**.

You will not find this insight taught in schools. This mysterious insight is only learned with experience. And experience of something never known is exceptionally hard to acquire.

This girl is not the first, nor the last, to awaken to this knowledge. But she was called to share her journey and story to you, that you might follow her steps to begin your own journey to discover the magnificence that lies within you. This magnificence will spread light in the world and bring an unimaginable joy. But the steps of the journey are hard, dark, and lonely. God asked this girl, this woman, to share the steps and her journey so you might feel less alone on your own.

You might wonder where you are you going. Only you will know. The steps are the same, but the scenery and destinations are unique. What you must know is you will go to a place where you can live and be as you were meant to be. A place where you feel fully loved, fully worthy, fully valuable, and more than enough. Where you will finally be **fiercely cherished***!*

Finding & Knowing My True Self

As I began my journey, I knew before I could love and cherish myself, I had to learn about my true Self. Who am I at my core? What makes me unique and special and valuable in the world separate from the labels? Learning this next step would be an entirely new and sophisticated dance with the Divine. This excerpt from my book provides the receiving of this new dance:

On vacation one night I sat down to write about the question "Who am I?" I wanted to peel away the layers and labels provided by others and figure out who I, Jessica, really am inside, and who I was meant to be. When I tried to begin to write, I realized I really didn't know. I really wasn't sure of who my inner Self truly is. Without the labels, the life experiences, and the perspectives of others, I was totally lost on my Self and how to explain or define myself. I asked the following question:

"What is my true Self – how can I know it to be it?"

I immediately received the answer, "I will reveal it to you like a flower, one petal at a time, until we reach the inner being inside." Through prayer, I received the message that I would need to unveil my inner Self through journaling over the coming days and weeks. Like a flower, each petal of our personality, or inner Self, adds to our beauty and uniqueness. Likewise, our inner Self must be revealed to us one petal at a time – one element at a time – where we can appreciate what it is telling us and what it means for our life.

As a result, over the following weeks, each day or every few days, I would receive a new "petal" – a new message just for me from the Divine telling me who I am inside. These messages were beautiful, powerful, and transformed how I see myself. In many ways, the messages – each petal – were things I knew about myself already but could not articulate or explain. They each certainly contribute to my unique soul and being on this earth.

During this time, I was also going through one of the greatest struggles in my life – the decision to respond to a new calling or stay in my current life as I had built and planned it. This struggle played out around each of these petals helping me to understand myself. And, by better understanding myself, I could better discern what I wanted in life for my Self. Rather than trying to figure it out for the person I thought I was, the person I had created in response to my experiences, I could begin to figure it out for my true Self.

If you are like me and struggle to articulate who you are – your inner Self – I encourage you to follow this practice. Visualize yourself as a beautiful flower, and each day ask yourself for one petal of your inner Self. On some days this will come easily and you will be amazed by your insight. On other days, you may not get anything, and that is okay. Sometimes we need more time with each petal before receiving the next. We need time to understand and reflect on what we have learned about ourselves before we can move to our next insight. Be patient and wait for each of these insights to come through – they will be very valuable and impactful for your journey.

My inner Self, my flower, and my petals have helped me better understand and value my true being. Here is what was revealed to me about my Self.

Petal One: You are an intuitive and insightful being capable of sensing and knowing what will happen or what is needed. Trust yourself and your inner intuition.

Petal Two: Your love is pure. You have the ability to love so many. When you open your heart, the love inside is infinite.

Petal Three: You have the ability to see challenges and break them into pieces – to understand why people feel the way they do without taking on that perspective for yourself. You can feel empathy and still remain in a place of neutrality and objectivity to help navigate complex topics.

Petal Four: Through your struggles you have gained tremendous insight. You are strong, fierce, and gentle. You can overcome more than most. You persevere and never quit. You get back up again and again. You can bend and flex in the storm and survive rather than break. You are indestructible. You rise from the ashes.

Petal Five: You are able to sift through knowledge to find the golden nugget needed in that moment of time. You are capable of acquiring so much knowledge, holding the concepts in your mind, and finding the perfect moment to bring them forth to reveal their value.

Petal Six: *You have the talent to understand the words, meanings, and emotions of others and to translate this understanding for others. Your words are the perfect combination of story, data, and insight to challenge thinking, confirm and convey useful information, and help others gain tremendous insight and growth.*

Petal Seven: *You are able to simultaneously juggle significantly more responsibilities, thoughts, strategies, and projects than others. Traditional limitations do not apply to your mind. You can access more of your brain than others.*

Petal Eight: *You are able to advocate for those who lack a voice, fear their voice, or have never known their voice. You have the innate confidence to speak truth, withstand the reaction, and stand firmly in what is right, true, and full of light.*

Petal Nine: *You are able to remain calm, focused, and react quickly and effectively in a crisis. You can take command and control, communicate clearly, and deploy resources and actions with ease and confidence. Those who follow your lead trust and appreciate your direction and guidance.*

Petal Ten: *You have a strong internal love for humankind and the world. If you could protect, care, support, and help them all you would do so. But you easily become overwhelmed and struggle with how best to contribute or take action. You long for big, massive change rather than small, incremental change.*

Petal Eleven: *You are connected to God and the Divine. You can hear their voices and visit them in your visions. You can move between worlds and bring insight, understanding, and truth to those who cannot.*

Petal Twelve: You are a creator, a creative being, capable of bringing tremendous love and light into the world. You were always meant to create – art, writing, groups, teams, projects, programs, ideas – your essence is to create. Your purpose is to create. Your innate creativity is a gift to the world and to others.

As you have unveiled and revealed the petals of your inner Self, you have found the Self you've always known but never named. The Self you've felt but never seen. The Self you knew was there but never heard. The Self you've ignored rather than valued. The Self you criticized and judged rather than acknowledged and respected. Now you must learn how to see, hear, value, and respect that inner Self.

You must see her for who she is in all her wonderful uniqueness. You must hear her over your thoughts and the judgements of others. You must value her above all others. For if she is suffering, you will have little to give. You must respect her existence, uniqueness, voice, purpose, and path. You must treat her better than you have treated anyone ever before. Shower her with love, praise, care, connection, and joy. Wrap her in a golden cloak that shows her value and her place of importance in your life.

Unraveling our Hearts

On the journey to love ourselves, it should come as no surprise that our hearts play a crucial role. I read once that love is universal—every culture, every community, every group has love. We feel love in our hearts, but we often create worries and fears about love—about having enough love, fearing the loss of love, or dreading we will never be truly loved. Another step in the dance of the Divine is learning about why we struggle, and I received the most beautiful message about why our hearts struggle with love. Here is the excerpt of this message from my book:

The heart gets tied up with knot after knot. Tying them is easy, untying them is not.

We tie them to try to hold the broken pieces together. We get hurt by someone we trusted and a crack in our heart forms. The more hurt, the more cracks.

So, we tie our heart up to hold it all together.

But each tie also prevents our hearts from growing.

We become stuck, held back by the knots that are holding us together.

Our hearts cannot expand the way they were meant to. Worse, we cannot give the love we are able and meant to give.

Our kids will never receive the love that was possible.

Our world's capacity for love is forever halted by each person who ties up their heart.

The act of tying up the heart, holding it all together is a natural reaction to pain and one we've been modeled and continue to model to our children.

But it is not how we were meant to respond to pain. Pain should create strength.

By demonstrating love – expanding our love of ourselves, others, and the world – while feeling pain, we will not only move through but also strengthen our resistance to pain and tolerance for pain itself.

In so doing, we expand our hearts and our capacity to feel and give love.

God is love.

We cannot truly feel God until we are expanding our ability to love. Expansion comes through pain.

For love during and in response to pain creates tremendous strength.

And as we do this, as our children see this new way, we will grow and expand and become closer to God than we ever before believed possible.

My dance with the Divine taught me to cut the ties that held my heart together—to trust God to keep my heart whole as I allowed it to fully expand and strengthen. You know the haze you feel when you first wake up? It's that moment before you become fully awake—when everything feels fluid and fuzzy. A life without this kind of love is like living in that haze—neither fully asleep nor fully awake, but trapped in the space between. Once you realize you are no longer asleep or in a dream ,you must awaken fully to fulfill your destiny.

As I danced these steps with the Divine, I experienced a complete internal transformation of my soul and being. As I learned and grew through the dance, I gained strength and sophistication. Through this strength, little by little, my life too is being transformed. My path and journey are shifting to an entirely new and beautiful direction.

This second book, unlike the first, required me to not just receive but experience and grow from what I received. When we grow and change, sometimes parts of us are no longer needed or elements of our life no longer serve us as they did before. For me, this dance with the Divine awakened knowledge deep in my soul of what it feels to be loved unconditionally by our God. And, as a result, how to love ourselves and others in the same way as the Divine loves us.

Once this love is awakened, we feel fuller, more joyful, more purposeful, and called to something much greater. For me, I felt called to follow the Divine's inspiration, guidance, and visions for my life.

Evolving to Exceptional – My Calling

The calling I received to create a new business named Evolving to Exceptional is still in its infancy. I've only just taken the first few steps to follow God's direction and dance this latest dance with the Divine. God has given me a few of the steps to the dance to begin my work, but I have yet to see the full performance.

As you receive from the Divine, the timing, the relationship, and the connection between concepts is rarely readily apparent. The message appears but why it matters or where it fits may not come for quite a while. But you can always trust it's as it was meant to be, even though it may not become clear to you until you are ready.

With tremendous fear and trepidation, I've stepped forward on this new and different journey for my life. I've created this business to help people live exceptional lives and to create exceptional workplaces for them to do so. As I begin to learn this new dance with the Divine, I can begin to see how I will bring my love, worth, and value out into the world.

I can see how my experiences can help others to step into their experiences. I can see how learning to dance with the Divine can create the transformation we all long for in our lives. And I can see how my dance with the Divine has awakened tremendous love and opportunity in my life.

As I complete this chapter, both literally and figuratively, I see only the infinite possibilities created by dancing with the Divine—the possibilities for bringing greater love, joy, peace, and happiness into the world. I see the tremendous experiences I will have as I continue to dance each new dance with the Divine, receiving such beauty and achieving only that which brings the world closer to God.

Have you heard the music of the Divine? Have you heard it as the wind blows through the trees, as a storm cracks with thunder, as the birds sing and the water flows? Have you felt the music just there beyond your reach? The Divine wants to dance with you. You need only turn on the music of your life and take the first step!

What insights, inspiration, and ideas came to you while you read this chapter? Make some notes below:

_____

_____

_____

_____

_____

_____

_____

_____

_____

_____

_____

_____

_____

_____

_____

_____

_____

_____

_____

_____

_____

Chapter 17

I AM ALOHA ✦

By: Theresa Meleisea

I am here, adding my story to this book, because of a choice I made in a crisis center on a Thursday afternoon at 3:33 pm.

I am blessed to be the daughter of two Polynesian fathers. My beautiful mother hailed from Illinois and passed in 2002. She met my Samoan dad, who hails from Aleipata, Samoa. They got divorced and she went on to marry my Tongan father who hails from Vavau Tonga. As Polynesians, we recognize the importance of claiming our connections to the land we hailed from, as well as our family lineage.

I was born in Oakland, California, but we lived in Samoa when I was a child. I love my culture and connect to both Samoan and Tongan traditions. It is a bit ironic though, because, while I firmly hold on to my culture, there are many ways in which I am not traditional. That is something I struggled with while I grew up, but I now see it as a blessing.

Growing up with three strong-minded parents (who came from a long line of strong parents) helped me become the strong, powerful person I am today. But it seems that every strong person gained their strength from overcoming their struggles. I am honored to share with you a portion of my struggle and how that has helped shape me.

I didn't know it at the time, but I see now that the entire Sunday was a series of miracles. That day, I was meeting with a man who was considering buying a car I was selling. The car wasn't mine but the person to whom it belonged had already moved away, leaving me with the car and a lot of other things to handle. My stress and anxiety were through the roof. I had weaned myself off the medication the doctor had prescribed me and I was self-medicating on a street drug that was not kind to my brain or nervous system. Getting off one drug and onto another so quickly had catapulted me into an extremely dangerous frame of mind.

My Samoan dad called me out of the blue that morning while I was in the middle of this big mess—cleaning up after my friend. Cleaning up after others was something I was really good at because I am the oldest of my siblings. I have been doing it most of my life.

But my dad was prompted to call me that day—making it my first miracle. He asked me if I was okay and I told him I was. That was a lie. He asked me if I needed money and told me that he would send it right away, but I knew there was no use for money where I was going. I knew I would soon leave this earth so I declined his offer. I was grateful, though, for the moment to say goodbye and tell him that I loved him, knowing it was going to be the last time I would be able to say it. There were tears in my eyes as I ended the call.

I had spoken to my brother-in-law the day before and I'm not sure what he knew about my big decision, but I could tell he was worried about me. He asked me to let him send an Uber so I could check myself into the emergency room, but I told him I needed another day to handle the mess I was in. That night, however, I wrote a goodbye letter. Even though I had agreed to go to the ER, I knew that nothing was going to change my mind.

But there I was the next day, that fateful Sunday, speaking to man interested in the car. I, along with the brother of the person who owned the car, was trying to answer questions about the vehicle when my brother-in-law called. He wanted to make sure I kept my promise of going to the emergency room. But his call only added to the stress and pressure I was already under and I began to be very confused and almost incoherent. I remember making eye contact with my friend's brother and I knew his eyes were telling me, "Come on, we have to sell this car! Get off the phone!" He didn't know that my goodbye letter was sitting in a closed envelope on my laptop, placed there for him to find after the deed was done.

I had decided not to do it at the apartment, because I didn't want him to be scared of coming home. To my mind at the time, this all made sense. I said goodbye in that letter, in all the right ways, so my family would know to love themselves. They would learn from my mistakes—at least, that's what I told myself.

I found that letter a few years later. I didn't have the courage to open it. I put it away until I had the courage to read it. To my surprise, everything in that letter was me speaking straight to me. I had written the letter to tell those I loved to love themselves, but the one who needed that message the most was me.

On that Sunday, as my brother-in-law pleaded with me for my address, I realized that I really needed to ask him to tell my children that it was an accident. I could not bear the thought of them knowing I had done this on purpose. But, with everything happening at once, I just gave him the address so I could get off the phone. After we were done with the car, I walked into the bathroom and put the straight razor away because I didn't want the hospital to take it from me. I would grab it when I got back. My friend's brother kept asking me questions about things in the apartment that needed to be handled, but I knew an Uber was on the way. I told him that I'd be back in a minute, and I went to meet the Uber.

I was confused about lots of things that day, but the one thing in my mind that I was clear on was that I was going to take my life and nothing would change that. Even though I had agreed to go to the ER, I was standing firm in my choice. I had even done my research. I had made sure the razor was sharp enough for the artery wall and I knew exactly where to use it. I knew it wasn't going to be easy, but I wasn't afraid. I just wanted it to be quick.

I was in Washington and, while it's beautiful, it felt far from home. As I sat in the Uber on my way to the ER, I began to feel sad for my daughter and my boys. They had no idea what I was about to do. I concentrated really hard, trying to stay calm, but the thought of my kids being sad made tears begin to flow. The hospital I was taken to had no emergency room, and I remember telling myself that if the Uber driver left me there, I would walk into the forest behind us and get it over with. But the Uber driver must have realized I was trying to check myself into an emergency room, because he told me that he knew where the ER was. I told him he could leave me here if he wanted to. I told him that I'd be fine. But he drove me to the ER anyway. That was miracle number two.

When I arrived at the emergency room, I walked up to the desk clerk and told her, with tears in my eyes, that I wasn't okay. She looked at me, nodded her head, and asked me to sit down. I'm sure I gave her my name and information but I don't really remember any of the words that were said until I found myself in a room with a psychiatrist. He asked me a series of questions and I answered them honestly.

"I agree," he told me. "You're not okay. We're going to get you checked in." He told me they didn't really have a psychiatric unit, so I'd be put in a holding station until I could get checked into a place nearby.

The temporary holding station didn't have enclosed rooms. It felt like a garage or a warehouse. I was lying next to a person who was wailing for no apparent reason. The wailing continued for at least an hour and a half. I could hear another person across the hall yelling, "Help me! Help me, somebody help me!"

I remember closing my eyes, taking in all the sounds, and thinking to myself, "Yeah, this feels about right." All the yelling and wailing was what my soul wanted to do, but I was stuck in this body that was trying to pretend like everything was okay when it wasn't. I didn't know how to yell for help.

A few hours later, I was checked into a drug crisis center nearby. They had found the drugs in my system so they were treating me like a drug addict. I wasn't surprised when they checked all the items in my bag. I was placed in a receiving room where they watched me as I slept, allowing the drugs to get out of my system. They offered me Benadryl, which I declined, and the strict nurse had no more kindness for me that day. I was told to sit on the chair and try to sleep it off.

I did just that. I fell asleep in the quiet room with no wailing. The next morning, I was assigned to a bedroom with one roommate and told I needed to attend the daily meetings. At the morning check-in meeting, I met the psychiatrist, who asked me if I was still suicidal. I told her I was, and she asked if I knew how I was going to do it. I told her I did, and she asked if I was planning on doing it at the center, but I told her I would do it after I left.

Day after day, she asked the same questions. She didn't try to talk me out of it or say it was a dumb idea. She just wrote my answers down in her daily records. That began to have an affect me. She wasn't trying to control me or tell me how to live my life; she was just getting the facts. I liked that she didn't have anything negative to say. It started to make me feel heard in some strange way, and looking back now, this feels like another miracle.

I cried most of the time I was at the crisis center because my heart felt broken for my kids. I felt so sad that they would have to go on without me. I remembered how it felt when my mom left this world, and I knew I was still carrying a lot of unresolved guilt about what my relationship with my mother was like when she passed.

I went to every meeting I was required to be at but, though I was present physically, I never added to them. I mostly cried.

I would sit in the common room and watch people. One of my favorite people to watch was this time traveler. He would walk around, pushing an imaginary box that seemed to be on wheels. No one could see this box-machine, but he could see it, and he kept pushing the buttons. He talked to himself all day long about time travel, unbothered that others were in the room with him. He was in his own world. It was very entertaining.

We would all go outside a couple times throughout the day for a smoke break. I didn't smoke but I went outside to get out of the locked facility and breathe in some fresh air. I liked to be outside by the trees. One day, as I was watching the time traveler during the smoke break outside, someone that sounded exactly like him screamed from up the street. I couldn't see anyone, but the time traveler could hear someone yell "Hey," so he yelled "Hey" back. I looked around to see if anyone else was paying attention, but no one was. This moment was only between me and the time traveler. I kept that moment to myself, but it helped me understand that the time traveler was getting some validation in his crazy, little world. It probably didn't seem crazy to him at all. I smiled for the first time while I was there, which felt like another miracle.

Another person that I liked to watch was a Hawaiian man. Of all the places in the world, this Hawaiian man was there at the same time I was and he was just what I needed. Even though I didn't speak very much, he looked at me and made me feel at home, if only for a moment. If you have ever been to Hawaii, you understand the spirit of aloha, and when us Islanders see each other off-island, we know and understand that we are a part of that same spirit of aloha, no matter where we are. That aloha is inside us and a part of us, so him being there helped me remember and feel that. This was another miracle.

The most important person there, though, was a lady with purple hair who walked back and forth, having conversations with herself. She never really noticed anyone around her. I didn't know she was going to be so important until Thursday, because that was when I was sitting at a table all alone, crying. All of the sudden, she made eye contact with me, walked over, and slammed her hand down on the table. She looked directly in my eyes and said, "You can't skip class! You have to finish school!"

As she was saying the words, an overwhelming feeling of love came over me and I knew this was directed towards me for a reason. I was being told that I couldn't do it... I had made the wrong choice and I needed to stay and finish. She walked away and went back to her conversation with herself, and I looked around to see if anyone else had noticed what had just happened. But no one was paying attention. That moment was just for me. Another miracle.

I knew that I had to stay and finish this life. But I began feeling confused because I didn't know what to do. I walked back into my room where there was a bed and a clock on the wall. I looked up at the clock and saw that it was 3:33. I threw my hands up into the air and said out loud, "If I'm going to stay in this life and finish, you have to tell me what to do. I don't know what to do—you have to tell me." I cried with clarity and confusion all at the same time and I knew that I needed to call my daughter to tell her I was okay and that I was coming home.

I went back into the common area and, as soon as I sat down, I immediately began receiving images in my mind of a new crisis center. It was one with colorful food that we grew ourselves, because there is power, love, and healing to be felt while connecting to Mother Earth. There was live music and chanting, because we heal through sound and vibration. I even envisioned a round building with a garden somewhere in the center. The roof was clear and open, so we could see the stars at night. I saw a place where we could gather around a fire to connect and heal. It was beautiful and magical.

On Friday, a kind nursed helped me call my daughter. I told the nurse that I didn't know what to say, and she helped me find the words. That night, I went home. Before I left the center, the kind nurse told me she had one more thing she wanted to show me. It was a booklet and we went through it together. The booklet showed me the steps of getting to the point of suicide ideation. It explained all the steps that I had gone through and I was able to see and understand how I got to where I was. I realized that I could have prevented it, because there was a clear window of time where we can help people out of this ideation. The nurse then had me draw a picture of how I'm going to go forward in this life, and I drew an outrigger canoe with a sail. At the time, I didn't know the significance of that drawing, but my journey eventually led me to a healing group called Kaimana, where I learned the significance of that canoe and how it would lead me to my purpose—to show others that they can finish this life. But that's a story for another day.

It was late at night, but I called for an Uber. An angel came and picked me up. I don't remember her name but I remember her kindness and how she congratulated me on having the courage to leave the crisis center and choose life. We had the most beautiful conversation and when she dropped me off, I was excited to get home and take a bath. I wanted to wash off everything I had gone through that week.

My brother and brother in-law asked me to fly to Utah to be closer to them so they could support me while I got back on my feet. They bought me a ticket and I felt so confident that I going to stay in this life. But it was also a strange feeling. When I got home, I found the goodbye letter. I think my friend's brother had read it, because it wasn't the way I left it, but he pretended he hadn't when I called him to ask for a ride to the airport.

I can't explain how I felt that Sunday as I sat on the plane. I knew I was going to live. My soul knew deeply that I wasn't going anywhere until I was done here. The plane ride to Utah was very bumpy, and I could tell that fear was coursing through the other passengers, but I remember thinking, "You people have no idea how lucky you are to be on this plane with me, because I'm not going anywhere. I'm going to finish this life so nothing's going to happen on this plane ride. We're all good because of me." I still smile when I think about that plane ride.

This was only the beginning of so much healing, but now I clearly understand that there is a window of opportunity where someone can help stop another's road to suicide ideation. This is why I want to create a healing center of my own in the future—the one that I envisioned while I was in the crisis center in Washington.

I see all the miracles that kept me here. All of those miracles have shown me that I was never going anywhere—but I had to make the choice to stay. So here I am, a few years later—not perfect and not completely healed, but I don't think that exists. Healing is a journey, and it's where all the higher learning occurs. I began to be inspired and follow my intuition to the fullest, and it has guided me to heal myself, my relationships, and begin to build safe boundaries. I feel more empowered—more confident—and I know I'm a living testament that following your truth leads you to the best part of your adventure. I can honestly say I love who I am. I love who I've become. I'm not lonely when I'm by myself, even though I know that I'm never truly alone.

I'm willing to shout from the rooftops that I am here, I love myself, I am important, I matter, and I'm not going anywhere.

What insights, inspiration, and ideas came to you while you read this chapter? Make some notes below:

_____

_____

_____

_____

_____

_____

_____

_____

_____

_____

_____

_____

_____

_____

_____

_____

_____

_____

_____

Chapter 18

DISCOVERING MAGIC INSIDE

By: Kristin Merwin

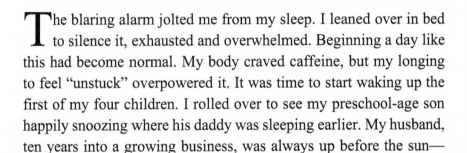

The blaring alarm jolted me from my sleep. I leaned over in bed to silence it, exhausted and overwhelmed. Beginning a day like this had become normal. My body craved caffeine, but my longing to feel "unstuck" overpowered it. It was time to start waking up the first of my four children. I rolled over to see my preschool-age son happily snoozing where his daddy was sleeping earlier. My husband, ten years into a growing business, was always up before the sun—working hard after little sleep.

I got out of bed, started the coffee, and ran all the days' activities and carpool demands through my head. I could feel the all-too familiar anxiety beginning to rise. Once the incessant thoughts ignited, my brain often struggled with "shutting down" its hamster wheel. Like many other moms, I was rushing and overcommitting most days, unaware of the growing disconnect within myself. My day would be filled with as much as I could possibly fit, with more spilling onto tomorrow's to-do list. I fell asleep that night pushing down the anxiety and hoping tomorrow would be easier.

My eyes sprung open, and I grabbed my phone. It was 3 am and I panicked that I wouldn't be able to fall back asleep. This bad habit was becoming my new normal. My phone chimed with notifications of new emails. I glanced at them quickly and the title of one message grabbed my attention. "Are you ready for change?"

Before I could talk myself out of it, I opened the email. I began poring over the words from a Life Coaching Institute. The sentences seemed to jump off the screen as I read about different programs to become certified in mind and body wellness. The email talked about creating more energy and processing emotion, relationship tools, and connecting with ourselves and those around us. My mind raced forward with dread, knowing that my oldest daughter would become a teenager soon. I'd heard so many horror stories of watching one's sweet kids turn into "aliens." Becoming a mindset coach had never crossed my mind before, but I wondered if it might be an avenue to learn coaching tools and dodge the impending train wreck of parenting teenagers. As I enrolled in the certification program at 4 am, I felt a surge of hope and excitement that caught me by surprise. I had no idea how one "yes" would guide me to say no to everything holding me down, working as a catalyst to more than anything I could imagine.

As weeks turned into months, I was jumping headfirst into the coaching curriculum. As I worked my way through each module of the certification, I wanted all the tools and immediate results. However, I was quickly learning that I had to first heal places within myself that I had once pushed away. As I tuned back into myself, I realized how disconnected I had become. Somewhere along the road to adulthood, I left parts of myself behind. And what I picked up was much heavier: the weight of others' opinions and the quest to earn love through perfectionism. These were all painful discoveries and I allowed myself to grieve the ways I kept myself small and molded myself to conform to outside opinions.

As the months passed, I continued to feel like I was "waking up." Occasionally I wrestled with the timing of everything and wished I had discovered this path sooner. Not one to waste good "mommy guilt" moments, I would struggle with how many times my own pain might have leaked into my family. And while I began this coaching certification to "handle" the upcoming teen years, it was the shift within myself that changed the entire direction of motherhood for me. Once again, my children were leading me to my greatest lessons.

While I did this work, I noticed my relationships were improving. However, the relationship I had with myself underwent the biggest transformation. Part of the certification process included learning about our "inner child," and how each of us reach adulthood but still have a kid within us. In the past, I heard bits and pieces of this theory, but it sounded woo-woo and not an avenue I was interested in exploring. However, because the Institute would be testing on it, I hesitantly peeled back the layers to learn about it. As the old proverb says, "When the student is ready, the teacher will appear."

I hadn't revisited that little girl within myself for a very long time. I used to feel like she was needy and whiny. I could easily ignore her with the bulldozing of the loud world. Growing up in a tiny town in Montana, I was raised by two parents who loved me and wanted what was best for me. We had a lot of extended family and friends, and you could often find us exploring the beautiful outdoors. My entire grade had only 40 kids, and most of us started kindergarten and finished high school together. This was my normal and I figured it was like that for everyone. As I returned to those memories, I realized there was so much more there. I felt misunderstood a lot and unable to give voice to my strong emotions and hurt. Generalized social anxiety plagued me but there was little awareness around anything related to mental health. I finished high school and went to a university in Montana until I ran out of money and drive. Years later (decades after I quit college), I would discover I had undiagnosed ADHD. After my diagnosis, so much of my life made sense. All those struggles and ways I tried to compensate were clearer now; I felt so much compassion for my younger self. I had accepted and embraced the course of my life but never realized the impact of trying to "keep up" and always feeling like I was behind. I also felt a lot of grace for my parents, who were trying to raise this precocious, strong-willed girl with her bottomless appetite for exploring everything.

Learning these integrative techniques and tools not only brought me healing but gave me a freedom that I had never experienced. After I was certified by the Coaching Institute, I immediately enrolled in another that specialized in working with children. I had learned so much from the first institute, but knowing the power and impact of our childhood was the most profound for me. I wanted to know more. How do we equip children with resiliency skills to navigate life's bumps? I knew that's where the magic is—reaching children before the world tries to mold them and dim their light.

As I continued the path of learning, I was still working as a photographer. Juggling photography sessions for kids and families allowed me to tap into my creativity (which I loved). However, I noticed that I'd lost a lot of the imagination and energy I used to feel as a photographer. As I completed the kids coaching certification, I began having inspiration to create something I had never seen before. The vision was so relentless that I did Google searches, hoping to find someone who was already doing it so I could allow myself to move on. This idea felt big, and it wasn't being offered anywhere that I could find. As I celebrated the new year of 2016, I began to create these ideas; I called them "Magic of Me" books.

My "typical" photo sessions were shifting. I now began with a questionnaire of what makes the child special and started to infuse each session with all the child's favorite things. From there, I filled the pages with personalized "I AM" statements to affirm their strengths and courage. If a child struggled with fear, I would remind them of their bravery. I would mirror an insecurity with the truth of who they are. Ironically, I didn't advertise that I was offering these books and only created them sporadically because I was stuck in perfectionism.

On my 40th birthday, I rewarded myself with an artist's retreat that I'd always wanted to experience. In the backwoods of Tennessee, I found incredible space to reflect on everything I wanted to bring forward. I remained quiet about my Magic of Me idea, not even sure that I'd share any of it with the other women attending. On the last day together, our host, an incredible photographer and artist named Joy Prouty, gathered all of us into a circle. She had us pull a random card from her deck (each containing one word) and explain what our word meant to us. The card I pulled was "dream" and a card fell from underneath that said "magic." Nervously, I poured my heart out to Joy and these women who had become like sisters to me. I explained all of it: the healing work, the certifications, the fear, and the deep dive to revisit my inner child. I told them about the power of a child seeing their beautiful portraits blended with these elements—it felt like nothing short of magic. The encouragement and love I received that day from each woman I had deeply connected with gave me the heart to expand this idea. I went home feeling more energized and equipped to create than ever before.

As I continued to move forward with Magic Inside, I was receiving feedback from mothers telling me of their children sleeping with their books, memorizing each page (before they could even read the words), and becoming inseparable from it because it brought them such comfort. Their messages sparked memories of my own childhood. My grandmother had lovingly created stories called "Magic Mountain" for each of her grandchildren. She personalized us into the story as the main character. They were handwritten pages, combined into a plastic 3-ring binder with page protectors, and complete with puffy stickers spelling out our name. We each cherished our Magic Mountain story. When my grandmother passed away, we all gathered to celebrate her incredible life. We remembered with delight and gratitude how much those stories meant to us and how our story made us feel special. Simple, yet so impactful. In many ways, I felt my grandmother's presence as I created the books for children. I realized how we minimize simplicity when it's often the most impactful. The last few years were opening my eyes to how guided I'd been all along. All of the people, circumstances, joy, heartache—it had all served a purpose. It was to help me grow and it had led me exactly where I was now. I used all of it to propel me forward.

In 2019, I had the opportunity to join an incredible women's mentorship. I had never done anything like this, but I was ready to expand Magic Inside and reach more children. With the help of my mastermind leader, Keira, I began to learn how to become a spiritual entrepreneur. I was realizing I still had some sticky, limited beliefs about myself. The women in the mastermind shared so vulnerably and we all grew as we learned to quiet the world's chatter and hear more deeply from the Divine. I had done the heart work and I had the head knowledge—now I needed to take action and trust.

Instead of looking outside myself for direction and answers, I began to remember the answers are within. Working spiritually allowed me to get into a creative flow like I had never experienced. In a fraction of time, I learned how to build websites, click funnels, and grow Magic Inside far beyond my original vision. I went deeper with the elements and pages of the children's books. I included letters from parents and role models, name definitions, double exposures with their spirit animal, and what the moon looked like on the night they were born. I created one for each of my children and experienced first-hand how special it is to celebrate your child or teen in that way.

On February 20, 2020, I officially launched Magic Inside into the world. I was so excited to begin a venture that had taken years of unfolding. I was blissfully unaware of the shift the world was about to experience. A few weeks later, news of an impending virus began to spread, and fear gripped every headline. We watched businesses and all my children's schools close. Public school kids moved to online learning from home. As weeks turned into months, we watched society's security blankets all yanked away. "No contact" became a rule of thumb as we waited to see what was next. It affected everyone and children were no exception. My daughter, a senior in the class of 2020, tucked away her unused prom dress and graduation gown. The promise of attending her dream university ended when they announced they wouldn't be opening campus in the fall. Feelings of frustration and anger began to boil within me. Media headlines felt very surreal with street riots and terror-laced predictions. I felt like I was back into survival mode. Had I done all of this to just fall flat on my face? What was happening? I also began struggling with one of my teenagers, who was drowning in schoolwork after several months of online learning and isolation.

It felt like I'd taken two steps forward and three steps back. Just as I had done years ago, I began to get quiet again and tune out the world's chatter. I turned off the news and tuned out those who were detrimental to my mental health. I hoped and believed I would receive answers and guidance in both motherhood and with Magic Inside. Soon, an opportunity appeared from conscious parenting expert, Dr. Shefali Tsabary. I had admired her work for many years and read all her books on parenting. Her Coaching Institute was accepting applications to become certified as one of her Conscious Parenting Coaches. The current struggle to understand my child was the catalyst I needed to apply. After I was accepted, I did a deep dive into the lessons and principles.

I was completely stretched beyond comfort. No one was more shocked than I to realize that it was not my child who was causing this divide and turmoil in our relationship. It was my own projections and suffering. The Conscious Parenting methodology peeled back all the layers and allowed me to see difficult truths and patterns within myself. Once I was able to see more clearly, I could heal myself and allow the relationship with my child to align. This transformation felt like a healing salve while our country was still wobbling in division and strife.

As the world welcomed 2021, all the problems and headlines of 2020 joined the new year. Reports of depression and anxiety in kids began to climb. Concerned parents and previous clients were reaching out with stories of the struggles their child or teen was facing. At times, it felt really overwhelming. I decided that, while I couldn't change the circumstances, I could choose to bring light into them. I had learned too much and sat in my own limitations too long to not throw out a lifeline.

I began offering mindset coaching for kids and teens. Because meeting in-person was not possible, I provided virtual coaching and meetings. I reminded myself that I earned my certifications for personal reasons and not to coach. I was doubtful this would all click for me. However, the amazing children and teens I was able to work with completely shifted any doubts that I once had about coaching. I was so inspired as I watched them grow and realize their strengths and divine magic inside. I was hooked! My only drawback: the curriculum I was certified in was awesome for in-person sessions but a struggle to make effective in virtual coaching. I knew there was a better option and by now I'd learned enough to trust and know that the answer would appear.

As I continued to coach the kids and teens, I became even more convinced that today's youth aren't victims of circumstance. They aren't merely "unlucky" to be arriving into a world that seems beyond hope. As I met with more and more of these strong, resilient spirits, I could see they were born with these gifts for such a time as this—here to bring the change that our broken world desperately needs. But even with extensive searching, I still couldn't find a curriculum that would work well for virtually coaching these kids. With that, I began to create my own online mindset program. As I moved forward, the lessons began to spill onto pages and complete lesson plans. "7 Magic Mindsets" was unfolding in perfect timing. A gifted artist, who was enthusiastic about the vision, created incredibly detailed characters to represent each of the seven mindsets. It became way more than I ever imagined it to be. I watched in awe as the characters of 7 Magic Mindsets began to take on a life of their own.

As Magic Inside expands, I believe the right team will join me in the future. We will equip qualified photographers nationwide to create Magic Inside portrait books for their own community and families. I'm building a podcast with free meditations and affirmations for kids and teens. I've created a kids' coloring book that normalizes mental health and understanding emotions. I was recently asked to consider the characters of 7 Magic Mindsets filming short animations to educate children on mental health disorders and help remove the stigma and confusion surrounding them. I believe that what is growing within Magic Inside is way beyond myself. I've merely been a vessel.

This past year has illuminated the deep importance of who we choose to surround ourselves with. I've let go of relationships that left me feeling drained and discouraged. I continue to join women's mentorship programs to challenge myself and stay accountable. I nourish and stretch myself with leadership retreats and time in nature.

I have also reconnected with Joy, and she blessed me with mentorship that felt so full-circle and powerful.

I keep my therapy "tune-up" appointments and joke with everyone that it's a gift for the whole family. I am a work in progress—a student first, and sometimes a teacher. Healing is not linear and I continue to seek alignment and joy within myself. While I have so many visions for the future of Magic Inside, I know that my presence is my power. As I ask for help, I'll always be guided to everything I need. I remember our purpose is not a pursuit outside of ourselves. To find our purpose is to unlearn all of our old programming so we can become who we are meant to be. When we do this, we reconnect with why we are here and live in the light and joy of who we are.

We discover magic inside.

What insights, inspiration, and ideas came to you while you read this chapter? Make some notes below:

_____

_____

_____

_____

_____

_____

_____

_____

_____

_____

_____

_____

_____

_____

_____

_____

_____

_____

_____

_____

_____

_____

Chapter 19

CORNERSTONES

By: Nicole McBeth

In masonry, the "cornerstone" is the first stone set in the construction of a foundation. All other stones are set in reference to this one, which means the cornerstone determines the position of the entire structure. My story has a cornerstone, and that cornerstone is my faith in God.

Eight years ago, I read an article that deeply resonated with me. It was a speech given by Jonathan G. Sandberg entitled "Healing = Courage + Action + Grace." His entire message on healing—what it is, what it requires, and what it can teach us—was enlightening and necessary, but there was one section that stood out to me more than the rest.

In his speech, Sandberg says that healing requires suffering, but it is a gift from the Savior. He poses the question, "How is it a loving God would allow us to suffer?" Sandberg goes on to share, "I have come to realize that my Savior cares more about my growth than He does about my comfort. One evidence of His love is that He does not spare me from the suffering I need for my development and progression, even when I get mad at Him. As a client once told me,

'I used to feel guilty for getting mad at God. Then I realized He can handle it.'" If there is one thing I am sure of after a lifetime of falling to my knees, waving my fists at the sky, and holding my head in my hands, it is that He certainly can handle it.

To know that I wasn't alone in "getting mad at God" gave me great comfort and hope. The journey of my relationship with my Father in Heaven has been as complicated as it has been rewarding. Sandberg's speech illuminated that for me in a new way. I had never read something that described my own feelings and my own occasional frustration with my Heavenly Father so candidly and accurately. I haven't forgotten it since, and I continue to share Sandberg's speech and these ideas with family, friends, and the people I coach. This speech holds a place for me and all my human imperfection, including my imperfect relationship with God.

My faith in God has determined much of my life. Prayer has been my collaboration with God—my default, my safe haven. This is where I have learned to really talk to God, spill my guts, and cry until I couldn't cry anymore. This is where I have run to in deepest gratitude for the miracles that have taken place in my life. Prayer has been my sacred space for countless years—it is my time for meditation. Prayer has truly saved me. It has comforted me when no one else could. It has been my best kept secret with my dearest friend. Prayer has been one of the most important cornerstones of my life because, in a life meant to test my endurance and faith, it has supported and sustained me.

I have not had a picture-perfect life. I don't think anyone has. That's not to say my life hasn't been full of goodness and joy, because it has. I have been richly blessed. However, it seems that nothing has come easy for me. I remember, as a little girl, having to wear special corrective shoes for most of my formative years. I remember the shame of feeling different for the first time. Those feelings followed me through middle school and high school as I navigated social pressures and relentless bullies. Thinking back on it now, I wish I could give my younger self a big hug and tell her it would all be okay.

I slowly gained confidence as the years went by, but I still had to work exceptionally hard to get accepted into the college I wanted to attend and then work even harder to get decent grades and graduate. I eventually achieved my goal of graduating with a degree in Psychology.

When my husband and I wanted to start a family, we went through years of infertility. Those were some of the darkest, most defeating years of my life. When we were finally blessed to get pregnant, our twins were born two months prematurely. We didn't have any family nearby and we only had one car so, against my doctor's wishes, I walked to the hospital every day to see my precious newborn babies in their incubators. Watching them in the NICU, being cared for by nurses, broke my heart. It's difficult to describe the helplessness and fear of watching your tiny baby fight for every breath. After two months, and with the help of a very compassionate doctor, we were finally allowed to take our babies home.

But that wasn't the last of my hardships. I have been challenged, tested, and tried through my hobbies, businesses, marriage, and the raising of our six children. I have run four marathons, but not without intense training. The struggles have always required so much exertion and effort—often more than I thought I was capable of giving.

But I keep coming back to God. He is my cornerstone because no matter what trial I have had, I have always been able to turn to God for advice and direction. God has helped my husband and I as we work closely with our youngest son—a tender-hearted, witty, loving boy who struggles with anxiety, depression, and suicidal ideation. This is about as unexpected, unrelenting, and unwelcomed as challenges go, but we find ourselves on our knees each night pleading for guidance on what is best for our son. And our son comes back to God too, even if just for the comfort of knowing he is not alone.

As consistent as the trials have been, so has my reliance on God, because that is the only place I have always found comfort, answers, peace, redemption, direction, and relief. No matter the setback, I've turned to God with my toughest questions, my deepest heartaches, and my greatest fears. Sometimes I turn in grief, sometimes in gratitude, sometimes in anger, sometimes in bitterness, sometimes in pain, sometimes with a lot to say, sometimes in silence, and sometimes with barely the strength to move, but always with faith that my Father is there.

Turning to God invites healing and growth, because it allows God to work with what I've got and what I can give. As I have gone through each trial, my relationship with God has grown and my understanding of patience has increased. Not all prayers have been answered. Some have even gone without response and others without acknowledgment, but my heart has softened and my spirit has learned to lean into Him more and fight Him less.

I can see now the growth that couldn't have happened without the discomfort. I see the fiercest love that only came by the toughest labor, and the brightest light that shines more brilliantly after total darkness. I see God stopping me in my tracks time and time again in order to guide me to something greater and transform me into someone better. He loves me enough to say, in one way or another, "Just hold on a little longer."

It has been incredibly validating to realize that, after so many years of trying and trying again, there is room for my imperfections, and even though my relationship with God isn't perfect, His love for me is. We've gone through it together, He and I.

I have learned that even when I wrestle with the Lord, I must also find stillness, recognize that His will is being brought to pass, and trust it. Some prayers have been years in the making, while others have been answered by God in ways that prove His power and reassure me that He knows what is best. Even in the quiet wait for His response, I have often found small answers and acknowledgment in the form of a call from a friend, an unexpected text, or the way the sun shines directly on me when I long for the warmth of its rays.

I believe God knows each of us intimately. He knows our deepest struggles, fears, inadequacies, and anguish. But He also knows our strengths, talents, gifts, and the blessings, insights, and connections that we need to grow.

I know without a doubt that there is a divine spirit, an all-knowing source of this world and universe. To me, that is God—the creator of all things, the beginning and the end. He is our Father in Heaven and He cherishes us, because we are His children. He wants us to feel joy, peace, and love in this life and He knows what is necessary for that to happen. He is simply waiting for us to turn to Him.

For those who are struggling to feel supported, seen, or heard—reach out to the Divine. Lean on Him. Collaborate with Him. Talk to Him. Share your heart with Him. He will hear you. I often find Him in nature, in the beauty of this world. I find Him in beautiful music or magnificent works of art. I find Him in the flowers, in the stars and the moon. He is in the infinite galaxies, the sun and the way it sparkles on the sea, the immensity of the mountains and the animals that inhabit them. He created it all and He is in it all.

Our twins that were born two months premature now have children of their own. Our four oldest children are married to four incredible spouses, without whom our lives wouldn't be the same (or nearly as much fun). Our family is a work in progress, individually and collectively, but I stand in awe of what our Heavenly Father has helped each of us work through and accomplish. We deal with anxiety, depression, and suicidal ideation daily. We celebrate each other's successes and ache for each other when days are rough. However, we start every day with new hope and new energy, and we have learned to give ourselves grace and patience as we walk through life together.

My mantra has always been: "If I can do it, so can you." I truly believe this with all of my heart. Take it from a girl who takes longer than everyone else to do just about anything—marathon training, articulating words, having babies, sharing my truth, and believing in myself... if I can do it, so can you.

I am sending love, light, and prayers for all who have opened this book looking for hope. You are meant to be here to fulfill your own unique purpose. You are so loved. If nothing else, let that be your cornerstone.

What insights, inspiration, and ideas came to you while you read this chapter? Make some notes below:

_____

_____

_____

_____

_____

_____

_____

_____

_____

_____

_____

_____

_____

_____

_____

_____

_____

_____

_____

_____

Chapter 20

THE DIVINE
NATURE OF CREATION

By: Ariel la Fae

Creation is a divine act. Without some aspect of divinity, creation does not take place. Items can be manufactured, and mass produced without divinity. With the proper Allen wrench, I am able to assemble an entire family room full of furniture, but I would not claim this as an act of creation. I may feel a sense of accomplishment, but I did not put into it the same labor I have when I have been truly creating.

In order to use the word divine to describe the creative process, it is important to understand how the word is being used. Religion tends to claim the Divine as its domain. I admit that this is an important aspect of divination, but for the purpose of this chapter, we are looking at divine in a more basic way that is easier to understand. The verb divine means to know right from wrong. A Divine Being, in the religious sense, is omniscient. In writing this chapter, I have purposefully been neutral as far as belief system goes. Please superimpose your own belief system onto my words, using what inspires you. Spirit whispers, qi flows, and the Universe guides. For a mere mortal to create, they must tap into the divine knowledge of what does and does not belong in this creation. Michelangelo once said that the sculpture of David was always present in the marble. He simply took away what didn't belong.

When Handel wrote *The Messiah*, he did so in three weeks' time. If I had the proper paper, I don't believe that I could even copy the entire score in that amount of time. He had done the preparation to already be a master composer, and he was able to divine what did and did not belong in this masterpiece that has inspired audiences throughout the ages. The music already existed, just as David was already in the marble. It took an act of divination to get this masterpiece from the ether onto paper so that skilled musicians could bring it to life. At the time, a live performance of the "Hallelujah" chorus moved the king (who bows to no man) to rise to his feet. One time I was attending a live performance with my daughter, and she asked me why the music made her cry. I told her that she was feeling inspired and that, in life, she wanted to have experiences that would bring her closer to that feeling and avoid experiences that took her further from that feeling. This is how we live lives of inspiration.

We don't have to be creating glorious works of art to create with divinity. Mindfully living inspired lives is a matter of divining what is the right thing to do next. Consider, if you will, the surgeon who is removing the appendix from a patient with appendicitis. Removing the infected appendix creates health in the patient. The skilled surgeon knows what to cut, what to leave intact, and what to remove. I'm told that of all physicians, surgeons are the most prone to developing a god complex because they are charged with permanently removing or altering body parts, and they must be certain that they are right.

What is right? What is wrong? What is true? What is false?

This is how I approach creation. This is how I live my life. Like the surgeon choosing whether or not to cut, I approach the creation of my life as a series of choices: what needs to be added, what stays, and what goes.

I used to be a lab assistant for microbiology at a local community college. I would mix media and create Petri dish-sized worlds to grow different microorganisms. In order to divine which microorganism was living in a specific dish for the final exam, students would perform different experiments to discover what the organism liked (or didn't like) in terms of temperature, media, pH, oxygenation, and so forth. I tend to think of microorganisms in terms of what makes them grow and what kills them. Sometimes, you want it to grow. When making homemade pizza crust, for example, you need to either use powdered milk or scald fresh milk (reducing 1 cup down to ¾ cup to kill the enzymes that inhibit the growth of yeast) or else the crust won't rise. In this case, yeast is a leavening agent. Other times, yeast is an unwelcome guest—an opportunistic infection following antibiotic treatment. It all boils down to what belongs and what does not. This is where divinity, knowing right from wrong, begets creation.

What comes first? What comes next? What belongs? What doesn't?

Journeys of self-discovery often have an aspect of creation built into them. This is purposefully done to encourage us to be open to divine inspiration. Arts and crafts are done at summer camp. In survival-type adventures, the ability to create a fire is not only an act of creation but is needed for survival. There is an entire branch of psychotherapy devoted to using art as a medium for self-discovery and self-exploration. The creation of the individual tells the story of what is needed to heal. The act of creating the art helps the skilled art therapist to guide the client on the road to clarity and recovery. Just like the presence (or absence) of purple on a Gram stain gives the microbiologist information about the cell wall of a bacterium, the presence or absence of color in a picture tells the therapist what the client needs in order to thrive. It is an act of divination.

In life, there are different decisions that we make that may seem trivial at the time but, in hindsight, we see that one decision changed the course of our lives in a profound way. When I was a senior in high school, I was flipping through the course schedule for my upcoming fall term in college. One of the first pages I saw listed was American Sign Language (ASL) classes. I thought it sounded fascinating. My parents disagreed with my decision. I had taken Spanish in high school, and my parents pointed out that there are many jobs where being bilingual in English and Spanish gets you more money. I was undeterred. The semester I started college, the university I was attending decided to accept ASL as meeting the foreign language requirement for graduation. I continued in ASL and my final upper division class was a three-hour lecture conducted completely in ASL. The actual title of the class was Deaf Culture, but it could have been titled How to Raise a Deaf Child. Fourteen years after I decided to learn ASL, my twins were born. One of them was deaf.

Speaking of my twins, like many multiples, they were born prematurely, and breastfeeding didn't come naturally to them. It was important to me to make sure that they had the benefits of my breastmilk but, at the same time, my production was nowhere near what was needed to feed two babies. I had read that homemade beer was great for milk production because of the brewer's yeast. As a new mother, I didn't have the time or the desire to take up the brewing of fine ales as a hobby, but I did add brewer's yeast to my diet. I was able to increase my production to 16 ounces at a time— enough to save up frozen milk. I remember the first time I filled two 8-ounce bottles in one sitting. I was strutting around like Tom Hanks in the movie where he is stranded on an island and was finally able to create a fire. "Look at what I have created!" Increasing my milk production was an act of creation. I had to divine what would increase my production versus what was inhibiting it. In addition to the nutritional aspect, I meditated, used mental imagery, and took advantage of the pheromones my babies gave off in the form of smelling one of their blankets as I pumped.

My husband, David, and I have been married for over 20 years. One time when our twins were toddlers, we were visiting his family in another state. One of our daughters has hypotonic cerebral palsy, and she had not yet started walking because her joints weren't stable enough. We were driving past a strip mall, and I pulled off the road. I drove to a shoe store, and I announced that I was going to go into this store, find a pair of pink high-tops for our little one, and that they would be on sale. We had been searching in vain for tiny high-tops for her for months. Divination—knowing what was there—manifested a way for our daughter to have the ankle support she needed to learn to walk. I had never been in that store before, and I have not been in it since. Over the years, David has learned to just go with it when I make such announcements.

In 2020, different people were doing different remodeling projects at home. Many homeowners were dismantling their '70s style fireplaces and giving away the decorative rocks that they now had lying about. I started collecting them for a large project that I was going to be creating. I should clarify that I sent David to various homes to collect as many rocks as he could of different styles. The first style was lava rock. We had a huge pile of black rocks for no real reason. Other remodels had granite counter tops being removed. I (David) collected several of those as well. David would ask me if we were redoing our kitchen, and I would respond that I didn't think so. I can understand David's frustration with the process because I have felt it as well. It is difficult to walk confidently down a path when you don't know where it leads. I collected other items like an industrial spool, a marble table, and different brass animals. I also picked up some leftover copper from a construction project.

One day, it finally dawned on me what we were making. After months of knowing that I needed items but not knowing why, I knew that we were making a medicine wheel and a fire circle. The granite counter tops became benches around the fire circle. The spool and marble tabletop became the center of the medicine wheel, with the copper wound around it to magnify the energy present. The brass animals represented different archetypes. The different types of rocks represented the four elements of the medicine wheel. Lava represented fire. Various pieces of granite represented air. River rocks were placed to represent water, and we used red rock for earth. Our medicine wheel was set up with an Incan cross made up of the four elements. We buried selenite wands at the four directions, and I read the story of the earth's creation as written in Abraham to dedicate the medicine wheel to benefit our family and help us feel connected to the earth and each other. It is dedicated as sacred space.

In the process of creating our medicine wheel, I learned more about my family and my family learned more about me. David had always wanted to set up a place in the backyard to meditate, but he was afraid of what I might say to the idea. In becoming more connected to our backyard, we have become more connected to the land. We have started to be more engaged in the growing of plants, and we have birds that live in our trees outside, as well as some domesticated birds that now share our home. We have a tree in our yard, which now has birds year-round. That didn't happen before we dedicated our land as sacred space. Our neighbor, who is a landscape architect, has commented on the change.

We listen, follow, divine, and create. This is living the inspired life.

What insights, inspiration, and ideas came to you while you read this chapter? Make some notes below:

_____

_____

_____

_____

_____

_____

_____

_____

_____

_____

_____

_____

_____

_____

_____

_____

_____

_____

_____

_____

_____

Chapter 21

YOUR STORY

This chapter is for you.

This chapter is set aside for you to share *your story*. Where in your life have you collaborated with the Divine? When did you hear God, or feel your angels support you? Have you experienced the love of the Divine Mother wrap you in Her warmth? Or, have the healing powers of Christ transformed your life? What story is the loudest for you?

And if you don't have a story yet, then this is the time to create one! Sit down and write out the life you want to live, where you collaborate and commune with the Divine.

Before you begin to write, I invite you to find a place where you feel safe, cozy, and at peace. Then send out the prayer that your angels will be there with you to hold the space in sacred light. After that, *ask God to write through you*. Imagine a beautiful light above your head pouring down through your body and out your fingertips. This light is a cleansing agent and also the medium in which you will receive. As you do this, the mind quiets and the soul will become louder.

Allow this story to flow through you as a witness of the Divine connecting to you, here and now.

Let it begin…

Thank you.

Thank you for sharing your story here. I may not be sitting next to you reading your chapter, but I honor you for filling these pages with your story. I now invite you to truly honor yourself for taking the time to write it.

And know that this practice is one that you can do over and over again. The practice of prepping and then asking God to write through you.

This is the sacred work we are blessed to participate in with the Divine.

Chapter 22

TAKE MY HAND

By: Keira Poulsen

D o you remember being little and grabbing your mom's hand as she led you through a crowd? She led you through a throng of people you didn't know to a location you could've never found on your own. Think about the amount of trust we had as children— trusting that wherever we were being led was exactly where we needed to go.

I don't remember ever questioning if my mom turned on the right street to get to the grocery store. I never wondered if we had missed an important stop on our journey. I simply grabbed her hand and allowed her to guide me.

As adults, we often think that we are always in charge. It is natural to feel that we must do it all alone. We feel that we must come up with the solutions to all of the problems that we face. This creates massive amounts of anxiety, stress, overwhelm, and loneliness… all of which are not necessary.

As you read through the 18 different stories in this book, my hope is that you found yourself in one or more of them. I pray that these stories reminded you that you are not alone. None of us are.

And even more powerful than knowing that we are not alone is knowing how taken care of we are by the Divine.

The solution to any problem is only an "ask" away. The support you need can be given at any second in any location as you ask the Divine. God is saying, "Take my hand, and I will lead you."

Reach out and take God's hand. Allow God to guide you in all things. Allow God to guide you on what to make for dinner, how to talk to your kids, spouse, or parents, and ask how you can be an agent for good in this world.

Ask, and God will guide.

Have you ever held a child's hand and tried to guide them when they wouldn't move their feet? If you are a parent, then I know that you know what I mean. It is laughable how impossible it is to get them to move. When that toddler digs their heels into the ground—no matter how determined you are—it isn't happening. The child must move their feet for you to be able to lead them anywhere.

And so, it is with us; we must take action first. We can reach out and take God's hand, but if we do not move our feet and take action, it only leaves us frustrated and motionless.

Receiving from the Divine has a remarkable energy of light and momentum. But, when we don't take action on what we receive, it can become heavy and weigh us down. We become the toddler who is sitting on the ground, refusing to move another inch.

That is when it feels like God is quiet. It is in these moments that we can feel like the Divine has left us to figure it out on our own.

The truth is that God does not leave us to find our destination on our own. He is just waiting for us to get up and start walking. *Action brings about action.*

If you choose to step in a direction, any direction, God can take that small, simple act of faith and turn it into a miracle. God, Christ, and the Divine Mother are all alchemists. They can take any matter and create something else. Our actions are like giving matter to the Divine to work with.

So, while God is tenderly inviting you to take His hand, it is also a request for you to stand up and walk.

You my friend, are needed in this world. Your light, your gifts, and your story are not meant to be hidden and tucked away. You are special because God created you to be so. God does not make mistakes—He creates perfection. From the whales who swim in the great oceans down to the worms who live in the soil of the earth, each creation that God has made is perfect and is here to fulfill a purpose.

You have a distinct purpose that only you can fulfill. And the more time you spend with God, the more you will remember it. This book is an invitation to live bigger, trust deeper, and create with God, *for God needs you!*

You are His hands, feet, and mouth in the world. When you commune and collaborate with God, you are bringing His work to be here on earth. You will create like you never knew you could. Your energy will increase tenfold and your joy will explode. God needs you to do the work on this earth to bring His light to the darkness. It is time to rise up and walk with God. It is time to say yes to the work that is here in front of you. As light creates light, share your light to awaken the light of those around you. Your life will never look the same for it will be made new in and through the Divine light.

May this be a cleansing of the old and an awakening to the new. May you reach up and take the hand that is extended towards you. Lift your foot and take the first step on this new path with faith and joy for what is ahead.

You are not alone. You are being Divinely led.

AUTHOR DIRECTORY

E ach author has put in a great amount of work in their lives to be able to write these stories for you. These women are also extraordinary leaders in their own way. I invite you to reach out to the authors in this book who you felt a connection with. Below is a directory of their names, their contact info and their resources. Many of these women have free gifts that they are sharing. I invite you to receive these gifts into your life as they will bring you more joy and light!

CC.ELAINE

Caren "CC" Johnson is a believer of intuitive living and unapologetic joy. As a speaker, storyteller, author, designer and entrepreneur she has been featured in countless publications and media outlets around the world, including: Say Yes To The Dress-Atlanta, The Woman Speak International Festival , Girl Talk-Atlanta, The Barbie Fashion Experience, Brides Noir Magazine, Ebony Magazine, Indianapolis Woman, POWER Magazine, E'lon Couture, WTHR Channel 13, Fox 59 News and The Indianapolis Business Journal; as well as numerous featured fashion exhibitions around the country. In addition, CC received the esteemed honor of being awarded the "Breakthrough Woman Award" for Economic Development by the National Coalition of 100 Black Women and the award for

Community Development and the Vision for a Prosperous Future by the Indiana Housing Authority.

Coming from a long line of dressmakers, CC birthed Cc.elaine Bride Chic over 20 years ago. Through her business, CC has had the privilege to make an indelible impact on hundreds of women, sharing wisdom, the energetic realm and spiritual insights. Her building of relationships and connections aligns with her ultimate goal of creating legacy and impact. Her knowledge and study of deep spiritual issues has led to her passion for sharing with others and offering practical insights to spiritual revelations. She is a believer of the imagination, as the source of how we are constantly creating our realities. With this as the foundation of her beliefs, whether on a stage or in a designer showroom, she embraces and teaches intuitive living.

CC he has studied the art of fashion in Los Angeles and Atlanta. She graduated from Atlanta's American College for the Applied Arts in 1991 with a Bachelor of Arts Degree in Fashion Design. CC now shares her passion for inspiring others to "Living a Life by Design" and correlating it with the demonstration of designing and creating a bridal gown.

She is the mother of 3 beautiful daughters and resides in North Atlanta.

Instagram: @ccelainetheweddingdresser

Facebook: @ccelainetheweddingdresser

YouTube: Intuitive Living Today with Cc.elaine
https://youtu.be/zubs5R68EiA

CAMI EPPERSON

Cami Epperson is a life-long seeker of Divine Connection. Never planning to be an author, she was living a fairly typical suburban life as a wife and mother of three children, as well as working a part-time job when she began her journey of self-healing and self-rediscovery. Soon she felt the call to write her first book. She has since left the part-time job to pursue her own work that is more aligned with her Divine purpose. Cami feels humbled and grateful to share her experience with you, as well as the relationship with Divinity that she has found within herself and with the Divine Mother. She feels it is possible for everyone to experience such a deep, personal relationship with Divinity.

Website: www.camiepperson.com

Instagram: @cami_epperson

ANGEL LYN, MSW

Angel Lyn, MSW, Soul Mentor, is a life coach, public speaker, and author. She focuses on principles of consciousness and spirituality related to individual growth, marital relationships, and parenting.

As a homeschooling mother of 5 sons, Angel became excited and passionate about continual learning, unlimited human potential and the process of personal evolution as she has watched her boys move through stages of development. She has taken from those lessons of observation and pursued her own life education and enjoys sharing stories and experiences that illuminate for others what is really true and possible.

Angel's mission statement is: seek truth, apply it in life, & share it with others. She is currently writing a book titled, "Soul-u-lar Evolution: a Mormon woman's transcendent journey to LOVE."

Angel hosts quarterly women's retreats, couples' retreats, in person groups and zoom groups teaching the principles of evolution that have led her to light-truth-love-joy-peace-freedom.

> **Website:** https://angel-naivalu-soul-mentor.business.site/
>
> **Email:** soul.u.lar.evolution@gmail.com

KATIE JO FINAI

Katie Jo is an artist, speaker, writer and artisan. Her passion is preserving the pathways of the ancients who lived in wisdom and harmony with the world around them. Making it simple, remembering our connection to the cycles around us, and teaching peace is a way of life for her. As an advocate, she hosts monthly events and annual training focusing on prosperity, Sound Healing Training, Reiki, Shamanism; and volunteers in Addiction Recovery, Human Trafficking Rehabilitation, Suicide Prevention, and Domestic Violence Eradication. When not painting or teaching; she's found hand-tying leather hoop drums or rollerblading down patchy back roads in her native Utah state. Mother of five and in love with the rascally Polynesian who married her.

> **Website:** www.KatieJoDrum.com
>
> **Instagram:** @katiejodrum
>
> **YouTube:** Katie Jo YouTube
>
> **Free Tutorial to Create Prosperity Crystal Grid with Katie Jo:**
> https://katiejodrum.vipmembervault.com/products/courses/view/1061290/?preview=admin&preview_access=1061290

KERRI ALICIA GALEA PRICE

Kerri Price is a SOULFUL High Vibe mama! A Movement Leader! She teaches moms how to VIBE AND THRIVE to heal their grief/trauma through lifestyle health habits, intentional movement, and emotional healing. She is a chiropractic wife and mom to 5 beautiful babies who are her most noble accomplishments. Kerri has taught group fitness for well over a decade, Fitness has always been a part of her life and human experience. She loves teaching and helping others move their bodies intentionally not only physically, but emotionally and spiritually. This is a radical mission driven experience that she is dedicating to the cause, to show up and serve you as a group fitness instructor and movement leader! She teaches that when you put the mind and body in motion, we begin to heal ourselves. It's not about perfection, but expression. Fitness is not only about how we look, it's about how we feel!! Tapping into authentic movement in the body has given Kerri the ability to create revolutionary movement through Grief, trauma and loss, and she invites and wants to give you permission to do the same. Life Transitions are inevitable, transforming is up to us, and through intentional workouts and exercises, YOU can give birth and find YOUR TRUEST DIVINE SELF AGAIN!

> **Website**: https://highvibemama.com
>
> **Instagram:** @_highvibemama
>
> **Facebook:** @highvibemama1
>
> **High Vibe Mam: Vibe & Thrive Podcast**: https://podcasts.apple.com/us/podcast/high-vibe-mama/id1553114933

MARIAH SLINGERLAND

Spiritual Counselor and energy healer, Mariah Slingerland has been on a never-ending quest to discover the secrets of the universe. What she discovered is that those secrets are deep within each one of us. Realizing the Divine was always speaking through her in the form of solutions for all those who were seeking counseling, healing, or mentoring.

Along everyone's journey there is a moment when assistance is needed. This is a pivotal moment. Knowing where to turn is essential, trusting the guidance is crucial and believing in the counselor is key. What you are seeking is already within you, and it's time to wake it up.

> **Website:** mariahslingerland.com
>
> **Instagram**: @mariahslingerland_

LIZ STONE

Liz Stone is a speaker, mentor, and passionate advocate to liberate the captive. Having been held captive twice in her own life; once at the hands of another, and years later by the unresolved fear, pain and shame, she now empowers others to create a life of Freedom, Dignity, and Purpose. This purpose is the drive behind everything she does including building The Balanced Stone, a healing center focused on trauma informed resources in Tooele County, Utah. Liz is also the founder and Executive Director of Empowering the One, a nonprofit that works in the prevention and aftercare of human trafficking in youth aging out of the orphanage in Haiti.

Empowering the One

Website: https://www.empoweringtheone.org/

Instagram: @empoweringtheone

Facebook: @empoweringtheone

The Balanced Stone

Website: https://thebalancedstone.com/

Instagram: @thebalancedstone

Facebook: @TheBalancedStone

AMY HILL

On the outside, I could give you credentials of what I do, but it doesn't really tell you who I am. I have been on an incredible spiritual journey of finding myself for the past 10 years. Here is what I do... I am an accountability coach for Freedom House Publishing Co. I am also an intuitive healer and practice in my home office.

Instagram: @amyhillclearblueintentions

Facebook: @clear-blue-intentions

SUZAN K. MANNING

Suzan K. Manning is a mother of seven children and grandmother of sixteen. She received a Masters of Professional Counseling and a Master of Education in her early 50's.

Suzan is previously published with: *"An Angel Stood Before Me: A Poetry Journal"*.

Instagram: @suzankmanning @treg716

Email: suzankmanning@gmail.com

VALERIE BOTE, RN, BSN

Valerie Bote is a Registered Nurse with her BSN from Chamberlain College of Nursing. She is a Transformative Nurse Coach receiving her training from the Transformative Nurse Coach Collective. She is a Holistic Wellness Coach with a certification from the Institute for Integrative Nutrition and a Reiki Master Practitioner, trained in the Usui/Holy Fire III system of Reiki. She started Life in Motion Healing, LLC as a result of her own journey. Her desire to comeback to self has brought her to her own quest for healing. Her mission is to cultivate a world that is empowered to love themselves fully so they may discover the healer within. As a nurse coach, Valerie partners with her clients to guide and support them in the work of healing the body, mind and spirit. She hopes to offer space where reconnection to self in addition to intuition and inner wisdom can be facilitated. It is her belief that true health is comprised of many factors; the choices we make in the areas of nutrition, physical activity, our relationship with ourselves as well as with others and our spirituality are essential components in our attainment of wellness. Harmony with the WHOLE body/self is vital.

Website: www.lifeandmotionhealing.com

Instagram: @lifeinmotionhealing

Facebook: m.facebook.com/ValBote22/

KEIRA POULSEN

Keira Poulsen is a mother to 5 amazing children, a spiritual entrepreneurship coach, author, host of the Awaken Podcast and CEO of Freedom House Publishing Co.

Keira supports women in understanding how to spiritually receive their books and create successful businesses derived from the message within their books. She does this through digital courses and in her mastermind - Awakening Authors the Mastermind.

She has created Freedom House Publishing Co. to bring sacred writing to the earth. These books transforming the world with light!

Keira believes that when women rise in their gifts, wisdom and power- they will change the world!

Website: www.keirapoulsen.com & www.freedomhousepublishingco.com

Instagram: @keirapoulsen / @freedomhousepublishingco

Facebook: awaken.keirapoulsen

Youtube: https://www.youtube.com/channel/UCvQk16owZqSv6uRmTh4hB5Q

Free Mini Course on "Creating with the Divine":

https://keira-poulsen.mykajabi.com/pl/2147541553

HOLLIE WARNICK

Hollie Warnick resides in the Arizona desert with her husband, children, animals and journals. She loves to play outdoors and discover new things. She is a Behavioral Kinesiologist, Reiki Master, Energy Healer, Coach and Author. Join her spiritual journey with classes, podcast episodes, or personal healing sessions. Check out www.holliewarnick.com or #behavioralkinesiology to learn more.

Website: www.holliewarnick.com

Instagram: @behavioral_kinesiology

Podcast/ Free Meditation:
https://holliewould.libsyn.com/the-gift-of-guided-meditation

RANDA STRATTON-DUTCHER

Randa Stratton-Dutcher is a life coach, digital course creator, retreat facilitator, singer/songwriter, soon-to-be author, cowgirl, mother to 5, and wife to her high-school sweetheart Aaron. You can hear Randa speak on her podcast "Going Dutch" where she discusses all of the above transparently. Randa loves to share light, messages, and assist others in reigniting the light that has dimmed over time.

Website: https://linktr.ee/randastrattondutcher

Instagram: @perfectlyimperfectranda

Free Forgiveness Course: https://randa-dutcher.mykajabi.com/offers/5pnDQZ5f/checkout

JESSICA TIETJEN, J.D.

Jessica Tietjen, J.D., is a spouse, mother, leader, lawyer, talent management professional, technology enthusiast, Gallup Certified Strengths Coach, an author, and consultant. After law school, Jessica began her career in the corporate arena expanding from legal to a leader of Talent Management and multiple operations functions. For over ten years, she shaped corporate Talent Management programs by creating strategies for peak performance. As a result, her workplace was recognized as a three-time Gallup Global Exceptional Workplace and four-time St. Louis Post Dispatch Top Workplace. Jessica wrote her first book, The Exceptional Life R-Evolution, to help anyone, in any role, in any place evolve to reach peak performance. She believes by reaching peak performance people can live their best life, an exceptional life. Her business, Evolving to Exceptional, works to make the opportunity to reach peak performance accessible to everyone by providing training, resources, tools, and coaching for individuals. They also partner closely with businesses to create exceptional experiences for their people. They specialize in supporting small to mid-size businesses to grow their human capital talent enablement strategies. Jessica is currently working on her second book, Fiercely Cherished Beings, and is the host of the Evolving to Exceptional podcast.

Website: https://www.evolvingtoexceptional.com

Instagram: @jessicantietjenjd

Facebook: @Jessica Tietjen

Freebie: Free First Chapter of The Exceptional Life R-Evolution: https://www.evolvingtoexceptional.com/firstchapterfreedownload

Free Reading Guide for The Exceptional Life R-Evolution: https://www.evolvingtoexceptional.com/opt-in-2ce0ca19-bc7d-4b17-ab5b-7ebf847df99c

THERESA MELEISEA

Talofa, my name is Theresa Poti, I have been a teacher of special education for over 10 years, I am a certified emotional process facilitator. I am a Kaimana graduate and cultural consultant candidate. I have a bachelor's degree in Sociology with the certificate in Ethnic Studies. I am of Polynesian descent, my father's village is Aleipata, in the district of Satitoa. I come from a long line of strong powerful personalities, with a gift of strong intuition and a deep love of family and community and cultural roots. As I stand before you, I make my mark in this world and I plan to leave a legacy of self-love, strength in unity, and empowerment.

Email: theresa823@gmail.com

KRISTIN MERWIN

Hey I'm Kristin! I was born and raised in a tiny town in Montana. I married a boy from my hometown, and we headed south in search of adventure and opportunity. A couple decades later, we still reside in Arizona, now joined by our four children and three crazy dogs. I enjoy traveling and I'm always looking for a new retreat or an outdoor challenge. While juggling carpools and kids' activities, I love to find pockets of quiet time in nature, meeting new people, and indulging my creative side. I believe that children can be our greatest teachers if we'll slow our roll and listen. Watching youth discover their magic inside and light up the world with their gifts is my most favorite thing.

I hope you'll join me in the Magic Inside Community – we are *just getting started* in helping kids become ALL of who they are.

Instagram: @therealmagicinside

Freebie: https://msha.ke/magicinside/

NICOLE MCBETH

Nicole graduated with a BS degree in Psychology, from BYU. She has always enjoyed learning about people's behaviors and social construct for why we as humans act the way we do. Nothing can prepare you for nor compare to learning about human behavior quite like being a mother to six children for over 29 years. In the midst of rearing their six children, Nicole decided to start a side hustle of baking cinnamon rolls for corporate 'Thank You's'. Currently, Nicole McBeth is the owner and operator of an organically grown online bakery called Cinnamomma, that specializes in confections and catering. She built this business on her tried & true family recipes that have been passed down through generations. She enjoys having one of her daughters, Cassidy Mantle, work alongside of her. Nicole's interest in returning to school to further her education as a counselor, or a coach, was a goal she always knew she would revisit when her youngest children got older. Previous to the world going haywire with covid, Nicole was able to enroll in a course and complete it, that has allowed her to now work one on one with clients. Nicole has always felt a special connection with, and deep empathy with people. She has been able to combine her unconditional love of people, with her open-hearted listening and her reverence of God to create an atmosphere that is welcoming to clients looking for gentle guidance in remembering who they are and their worth as an individual and as a child of God. Nicole loves spending time on the beach with her family, she loves hot yoga, walking, meditation, reading and of course cooking and baking. This chapter, Cornerstones is the second piece of writing Nicole has. Before this short essay, she had just finished her first little book called, 'Little Prayer', a story about her Granna as a little girl. Madeline McBeth Collett was able to help edit both writings, prior to publishing, and Cassidy McBeth Mantle was able to help with illustration for 'Little Prayer'. Travis and Nicole McBeth reside in Gilbert, Arizona. They have been married for thirty-two years and both feel like their family is their greatest joy. They will tell you they do not have a perfect marriage or family and that they are both a 'work in progress'.

> **Instagram**: @nicoledonai or @cinnamomma_ or @TheHealingHous_

ARIEL LA FAE

Ariel la Fae is an autistic author and advocate. She speaks at professional conferences about being trauma-informed in the workplace, reasonable accommodations, and the notion that autistic people are people, too. She has a master's degree in Deafness Counseling and has has worked as a counselor for many years. The nature of her work requires her to have a nomadic lifestyle.

When she is not traveling, she resides on Turtle Island with her husband and autistic twin daughters.

Watch for future publications: If you Stop Torturing us, we Will Stop Screaming; He Said he Loved me, and Other Lies; and The Queen is Dying.

Website: www.ArielLaFae.com

Facebook: Ariel la Fae or @ariel.la.fae.autistic.author.advocate

Instagram: @ariel.la.fae.speaker

Email: Ariel.la.Fae.speaker@gmail.com

Made in the USA
Middletown, DE
22 February 2022

61476940R00158